IS THIS BOOK REALLY FOR YOU?

This book is not for everyone. It was written for the solo and small-firm attorney. They are the backbone of the legal economy, their families, and their communities, but they often find themselves marginalized by their local and state bar associations, pounded on by the large, 800-pound gorilla firms, and taken advantage of by the marketing vultures pitching their wares.

If you are a solo or small-firm attorney, take a quick assessment of your life today. I believe that where you find yourself in your today is a result of your past decisions. If you're happy as a duck in the rain, you practice runs well, and you feel you're a hero to your family and an icon in your community, by all means keep doing whatever you've been doing, but read this book anyway. I guarantee you'll find a nugget or two here that will push you even higher.

But if your practice isn't everything you deserve at this point in your career, if there's stress on the home front because of inconsistent and disappointing income, or if you're overstocked with bad clients because you don't feel confident in turning them away (even though you and your staff know it will cause heartburn), you can choose to make changes. This book will help guide you.

This book was inspired by the thousands of lawyers who make up the membership of Great Legal Marketing, have attended our events, or who have been influenced by our marketing and practice-building principles and have reported their results back to us. Since 2006, we have been running a giant laboratory of marketing and practice building strategies for the solo and small-firm lawyer. Little by little, we're not only improving the lives of the lawyers who are our members, but we are also improving the image of lawyers in the community because the tone and tenor of lawyer advertising is changing.

RENEGADE LAWYER MARKETING

How Today's Solo and Small-Firm Lawyers
Survive and Thrive in a World of Marketing
Vultures, 800-Pound Gorillas, and LegalZoom

BENJAMIN W. GLASS, III

WORD ASSOCIATION PUBLISHERS

Printed in the United States of America.

ISBN: 978-1-63385-080-4
Library of Congress Control Number: 2015948516

Cover design by:
Sherwin Soy (sherwin@sherwinsoy.com)

All cartoon images in this book, including the cartoon on the cover,
are designed by:
Jim Huber (Jim@HuberSpace.net)

All ads shown are designed by :
Kia Arian, ZineGraphics.com

Published by
Word Association Publishers
205 Fifth Avenue
Tarentum, Pennsylvania 15084

www.wordassociation.com
1.800.827.7903

TABLE OF CONTENTS

DISCLAIMER

Hey, I'm a lawyer. I have to write a disclaimer, right? Besides, my publisher made me include this. Here it is.

This book is not intended to be legal or ethical advice. While I'm sure this book will inspire you, you should know that trying to copy one aspect of anyone's comprehensive marketing system without understanding what's going on under the hood can be dangerous to your wallet.

Any copies of advertising used in this book are solely for instructional and educational purposes. Any ad examples used are not to be ripped off verbatim by the reader. Certain marketing materials used in the promotion of my law firm, BenGlassLaw, may be licensed to members of Great Legal Marketing (GreatLegalMarketing.com). All ads for BenGlassLaw and Great Legal Marketing are designed by Kia Arian, ZineGraphics.com.

Legal requirements and ethical standards governing advertising, marketing, client relationships, and duties to clients vary from state to state. Only you are responsible for your own actions.

Neither the author nor the publisher makes any warranties, express or implied, about whether any of the marketing documents, materials, or instructions in this book are legally or ethically appropriate in your jurisdiction. If in doubt about the appropriateness of any of the materials or instructions, you should obtain competent guidance just as you would with any marketing documents, materials, or plans you develop on your own.

Throughout this book, you will find references to and opinions about other products, services, and vendors. Any opinions are those of the author only. It is your responsibility to use your own mind to determine if a particular vendor, product, or service will be right for you. To the extent you disagree with my opinions—write your own book and put it out into the world as I have done.

One cannot write a book about marketing without mentioning the Internet. The problem is that once you give technical advice about how to improve your Internet marketing, Google changes its algorithms and you may end up looking foolish because your advice becomes outdated. Remember key word "stuffing," getting an unlimited number of low-quality links, the "importance" of meta descriptions, and all the time we spent setting up our Google "authorship pages"?

In this book, I have stayed away from technical Internet advice to focus on how the general rules we apply to all forms of advertising media can be used on the Internet. How to attract, convert, and maintain clients and fans remains the same no matter what media is used for the messaging, and it is a mistake to think the Internet is different. For the latest technical information on web marketing for lawyers, we recommend you follow the advice Foster Web Marketing (FosterWebMarketing.com) is currently giving. Foster Web

Marketing is the only Internet marketing firm for lawyers that understands what is in this book.

Finally, I make no income representations here. Many lawyers who have been exposed to the ideas in this book end up taking massive action and reaping financial, emotional, and professional benefits. On the other hand, some will buy this book but, lacking true ambition, will never crack the cover. Whether you will survive and thrive in a world of marketing vultures, 800-pound gorillas, and LegalZoom depends entirely on your proclivity to take action, manage a law practice, and provide competent legal services. We think income inequality is a good thing because you are in total control here.

We have attorney members across the United States and Canada and in such far-flung places as England, Ireland, Russia, Australia, and New Zealand. In many places outside the United States, lawyer advertising is basically in the same state as it was in the United States before Van Osten got the "crazy" idea to advertise his legal services. In other words, advertising as we know it is basically not allowed.

If our members in Russia can figure this out, so can you.

Your Success is Dependent on the Actions You Take –
Which Lawyer do You Want to Be?

ACKNOWLEDGMENTS

I owe an enormous debt of thanks to all the folks who make my membership organization, Great Legal Marketing, possible, including Mairim Bartholomew, Charley Mann, Colin Lynch, Laura Vezzani, Kia Arian, Tom Foster, and Rem Jackson. They help get more things done than any of us ever thought possible. Together, we're changing lives.

Our solo and small-firm attorney members around the world are tremendous. They send me their most interesting legal marketing ideas, tactics, and strategies and permit me to comment upon and share them with members, recognizing that a rising tide will lift all boats.

You solo and small-firm attorneys are heroic figures and must be acknowledged and thanked here. You are the ones who are not only ensuring that legal services across the entire legal spectrum are available to everyone, but are doing it while dealing with the challenges of running a small business in a world that at times seem to be "against" both attorneys and small businesses. The weight of the world rests on your shoulders. You should be applauded by your communities, but I know most of you are not. I think this book will help position you as authentic "hero" in your town.

Of course, behind it all is my wife and best friend, Sandi. We met in 1977, married in 1981, and have been living life big ever since. Most of the "philosophy" you read in this book actually comes from the discussions that Sandi and I and our nine children have had around the dinner table for years.

Finally, I am deeply indebted to my friend Dan Kennedy (NoBSBooks.com), without whose provocation to "just do it," there would be no Great Legal Marketing. His advice over the years has been more valuable than even he knows.

To the vast majority who are not successful, it's a mystery as to why top achievers achieve. To the top achievers, the only mystery is why the unsuccessful don't emulate the behaviors of the successful. Most behaviors are observable. If you don't have personal, live access to a top achiever, your library is a great and free source of biographies and autobiographies of them.

—Dan Kennedy
DanKennedy.com

BUT WHAT WILL WE TELL THE KIDS?

If you're an experienced attorney, you undoubtedly get asked by young people from time to time, "Should I go to law school?" And if you're in law school, you may be wondering, "Have I made a wise decision?" Maybe you're thinking about going to law school and wondering, "Is that still a good idea these days?" Let me share the answer I give to all who ask me these questions.

> Thinking about going to law school? Good for you. The law needs smart people who can solve problems. There's a never-ending supply of clients, rich and poor, you can help lead through an ever more-regulated society. As times change, we need people who can protect individual liberties and the flow of good ideas, help people make practical decisions about their legal situations, and become heroes to their communities.

You'll have to think outside the box. Forget about going to the fanciest, highest-rated, and most expensive law school you can find; it's not worth it. Most of the people you'll come across in your career won't care what law school you went to. And the debt you'll incur going to an expensive law school may enslave you and prevent you from living a fulfilling, productive life.

You'll have to think outside the box in other ways, too, because most law schools are good at preparing you for a world that no longer exists. Instead of Law Review, you should take classes that tell you how to run a business, how to read a spreadsheet, how to get clients, and how to become influential in your community. Your law school probably doesn't have those classes. Mine didn't. But that won't stop you from enrolling in some business classes at a community college. Go ahead. Do it. Hour for hour, it will be far more valuable than Law Review.

I want you to know something else about your decision to be a lawyer: they can be heroes, and it's cool to be a hero. Lawyers can be heroes in many ways today. Sure, you help clients, and when they survive whatever challenge they face with you at their side, they will see you as heroic, but there's more. When you run a profitable practice that doesn't drive you crazy and allows you to get home in time for dinner and soccer and ballet and date night, you'll be a hero to your family.

Finally, when you not only survive but also thrive as a small business owner, you will become a hero to your community, someone who employs people, pays taxes, and is an inspiration for all the other small business owners in your community who are, after all, the economic engine of America.

I want to thank you for considering becoming a lawyer. We need people who can make a real difference in other people's lives. You just have to think a little differently than I did when I started my legal career.

Ben Glass

Benjamin W. Glass, III

YOU MADE A GREAT DECISION TO INVEST IN THIS BOOK!

In 2008, VB Attorneys celebrated its fourth birthday and several major victories. However, we were miserable. We were working too many hours, not getting the types of cases we really enjoyed working, and not spending any time with our families. We didn't leave big law to be miserable; if we'd wanted to be miserable, we'd have stayed.

I went looking for answers and found Ben Glass and his first book, *Great Legal Marketing*. I hadn't even finished the book when I knew we needed to change our mind-set and our practice. That we needed to spend more time working *on* the practice than *in* the practice and take back control of our lives from the monster that had become our law firm.

What I didn't realize would be so revolutionary would be what actually happened when we took control of our lives. That one concept—the mind-set that we were in control—changed everything, from how we took cases and how we created and maintained relationships with our clients to how we scheduled our time. Best of all, it radically changed our case outcomes for the better.

Taking control of our lives and our practice allowed us to spend more time with our families, to spend more time doing what we love, and to look like the guy on the cover of *Great Legal Marketing* for more than two months a year. We have, with the help of Great Legal Marketing and our web developer, Foster Web Marketing, drastically changed the way we generate cases and connect with potential clients.

In 2013 alone, we were featured in more than sixty national and international news articles and were featured in over a dozen national news broadcasts in relation to cases we were handling. We went from being a small, insignificant firm to the go-to firm for massive injury cases within five years. All because we were in control of our lives and our practice.

VB Attorneys is the means to living the lives of our dreams, but it is not in control of our lives. In five years, the concept that we were in control has generated over $100 million in verdicts and settlements for our clients. That mind-set is a $100 million idea, and it's all thanks to Ben and *Great Legal Marketing.*

—Brian Beckcom
Houston Maritime and Personal Injury Attorney
(VBAttorneys.com)

CHAPTER 1

GORILLAS, VENTURE CAPITALISTS, VULTURES, AND THE BAR ASSOCIATION:
THREATS TO SOLO AND SMALL-FIRM LAWYERS

The threats to the solo and small-firm lawyer are all around—yesterday's responses won't do. Even though you may be a good lawyer who's delivering excellent legal services in a highly ethical way, marketing your law firm to today's highly skeptical and better-informed consumer is more challenging than it has ever been before. The advertising you spent your hard-earned money on two days ago to get your message out landed on deaf ears because your next client didn't have his accident, find out her spouse was cheating on her, or get arrested for DUI until *yesterday*. Two days ago, their brains didn't register your message amid the thousands of other messages they were inundated with that day because they didn't have a legal need then. If you don't have squirrels running through your attic right now, you didn't hear the pest-control ad on the radio this morning, either.

Here's the problem: your next clients are bombarded with marketing messages of all types, and they have more choices than ever in terms of how and when they'll consume marketing media, including yours. Will they be watching traditional TV, reading a printed newspaper, listening to satellite radio, or searching for you on the Internet? If they go to the Internet, the simple question used to be which browser would they use? Today, you have to also predict which device they prefer. They will likely visit 10 or more legal websites when they conduct searches, and they might start on YouTube rather than with a traditional search engine.

Wherever they go looking, they will find that law firms abound in just about every market area, and a handful of them dominate the advertising media. These 800-pound gorillas often spend hundreds of thousands of dollars a month on the Internet, TV, radio, billboards, and advertising on buses. At first glance, they seem to be everywhere. The Internet itself has advertising not only from real law firms, but also from "lead capture" sites set up by nonlawyers who spend tons of money on "key word" advertising, only to sell the leads to the highest bidder. On top of that, you'll find "follow me" advertising that will keep showing a law firm ad to a searcher for 90 days or longer after that searcher has visited a law firm website.

The fight to be noticed on the web is fierce. As Google keeps testing and changing its algorithms, lawyers and other advertisers find that search engine optimization is almost a full-time job in itself. Tactics that worked six months ago to secure a spot at the top of search results may now be punishing your site, while the firm that launched a site last week may be at the top of search engine results, at least for now.

Maybe your next prospect will simply bypass the traditional lawyer route completely, opting instead to try self-help at LegalZoom, NextGen Justice, US Legal, Legal Shield, Avvo, or any of a dozen other "do it yourself" legal sites. In 2013, venture capitalists invested over $450 million in "self-help law," and over a million wills were written in one year at Sam's Club! Sure, these firms are selling just forms right now, but how long will it be before the entire process for no-fault divorce, for example, is cheap, consumer friendly, and efficient? Think companies like Amazon aren't thinking about this now?

Do you think your bar association is there to protect your small practice? It says it is, but one morning, lawyers here in Virginia woke up to find one of the local bar associations sending direct mail, on bar association letterhead, to DUI arrestees. The letters told recent arrestees not to hire any "out of town" lawyers and even went so far as to suggest that local lawyers could get better results in front of local judges. (Imagine if you said that in your advertising!)

The threats to our practices are all around us.

The marketing vultures, those selling you the next purple pill to save your practice from destruction by these threats, prey on your lack of knowledge about marketing, filling your email inbox and voice mail with pitches to "get new leads" through their proprietary pay-per-click schemes or "be found on the first page of Google." Their slick presentations promise the one-step solution to your problem: buy their services. Problem is, nothing as challenging as marketing a law practice can be solved in one step.

Nothing as challenging as marketing a law practice can be solved in one step.

THIS BOOK IS THE ANSWER TO YOUR MARKETING CHALLENGES

There is an answer, and that answer is to not just keep doing what got you where you are now. How well you respond to these threats will determine your family's financial future.

Improving your marketing is the greatest way you can leverage your time and capital. Lawyers who understand this take marketing—make that the *science* of marketing—very seriously. They realize the quickest path to making more money and building a more fulfilling practice is through marketing. They devote time, energy, and money to being the best marketers in town, and they are proud of what they do. Moreover, their marketing does not embarrass them, their families, or the profession.

Law schools are completely clueless about this. Sure, they're great at teaching you what to do once you get a client, but they seem to forget that none of that matters unless you have a good number of good clients. Lawyers come out of law school and enter the profession in a world that simply doesn't exist. Once they're there, their situation doesn't get much better as most bar association "marketing" seminars are nothing more than "you can't do" lists.

While educational opportunities for becoming a better lawyer abound, most lawyers spend very little time, money, and energy on developing the most important skill set any lawyer could have: how to acquire clients and get them to evangelize for you.

This book can fix that.

CHAPTER 2

AND DROP YOUR ENTITLEMENT MENTALITY!

Understand this: your being a good lawyer and delivering quality services in an ethical manner doesn't entitle you to anything. The market doesn't care, and the world owes you nothing for being a good person or for having chosen law as a profession. If you are young, no one cares about your law school debt, either. You have to convince your prospects that you're the right choice for them over all the other choices they have, including the choice to not hire a lawyer.

You may have a plaque that declares you "super."
The market doesn't care.

7

CHAPTER 3

THE SADDEST LETTER EVER WRITTEN BY A LAWYER

On January 1, 2014, the *Wall Street Journal* ran a letter written by a retired trial lawyer. He was commenting on the reports of decreasing enrollment in law schools. The *Journal* headlined the letter, "Some Reasons Not to be a Lawyer."

The author, Laurence Valle, of Miami, wrote that he had spent 43 years practicing and basically hated it. He reported working 60 hours a week in a profession that "the community views as a burden."

How sad. Mr. Valle never built any sort of a business. I checked him out. He worked as "of counsel" for some big, billable hour firm (ConroySimberg.com), no doubt grinding it out, hour by hour, 'till the bitter end.

If you, like me, have a journal in which you keep listing things you hate doing and want to eliminate, please feel free to write, "Work 60 hours a week in a profession in which no one likes me," then figure out the steps you need to take right now to build your perfect practice. Build a practice that brings you joy and in which you can take pride. Please don't tell me it can't be done in your practice area or location.

At Great Legal Marketing, we have members in virtually every consumer practice area, from coast to coast and border to border (and beyond) who have practices that excite them so much that they *encourage* young folks to go to law school because being a lawyer is a great way to make a living.

Build a practice that brings you joy and in which you can take pride.

How do you get that mind-set if you don't already have it? When I started my (then) solo practice, I struggled. I thought I had to follow a traditional ladder of success, which included (1) taking other people's crappy cases, (2) volunteering for a lot of bar committees, and (3) doing good work until they came. That's all I had ever been told.

What changed? Many people who know a *little* about me think it's all about my marketing techniques. It's not. I never start a public seminar or talk about "marketing techniques." What changed was the way I saw the world. I developed an entrepreneurial mind-set; I said, "Screw it. Some of these traditional ideas sound nonsensical. I choose not to go down that path. I don't care what anyone else thinks."

The impetus for that change was my now good friend Dan Kennedy. It was not, I think, just plain chance that I received his sales letter for Magnetic Marketing 20 years ago. I got that letter from Nightingale-Conant because I had sought out "success" information from that company. They led me to Dan, and Dan introduced me to the thinking of Napoleon Hill, Earl Nightingale, Maxwell Maltz, and others.

I started attending Dan's events and ran into more people who not only had the success mind-set, but who also impressed me as authentic, real people. As I got to know them, I saw that the most successful of them had much in common about the way they thought.

Mr. Valle is dead wrong.

Here's what I tell any young person who is thinking about going to law school.

1. Good for you. Our ever more-regulated world needs smart people who can solve legal problems. There will never be a lack of potential clients—any market, any location. When someone says, "There are too many lawyers" or "The market sucks," just smile, nod, and walk away.

2. Ignore most of what you hear in law school about what's allegedly required of you in the profession. I have yet to meet a law school professor who thinks about the practice of law the same way a successful businessperson thinks. (If you're that law school professor, contact me. I'd like to meet you. If you teach a class on the business of the practice of law, I'll give you as many copies of this book as you have students.)

3. As fast as you can, find a group of successful business owners you can hang out with. Some might be lawyers, but they don't have to be. Show

up. Listen. Be curious. Ask questions. When you hear a good idea, ask yourself, "How can I use that idea in my law business?"

4. Immerse yourself in the success literature. I'm not just talking about reading Napoleon Hill and Earl Nightingale. I'm talking about reading the biographies of real business leaders. How does Jeff Bezos think? What drove Steve Jobs after they kicked him out of Apple? What principles did John Allison use to build BB&T, and what ultimately drove him *from* BB&T?

5. Never believe your long-term fortunes are tied to anything but the decisions you make. Sure, we all experience setbacks, but that's why you should read the biographies of Bezos and Jobs and books like Scott Adams's *How to Fail at Almost Everything and Still Win Big.* Lots of people thought selling books via a website was a dumb idea.

6. Be principled. Decide what rules you'll live by and adhere to them. People really do want to know what you *stand for,* but your actions had better back up your words or they will lose all faith in *anything* you say.

Yup. The marketing stuff I teach works. But it works a whole lot better when your head is on straight.

CHAPTER 4

BANNED BY THE LOCAL BAR

"Ben, we're very concerned about having you speak to young lawyers." That was the gist of a call I got in 2014 after I'd been asked to speak about marketing to the young lawyers of one of the northern Virginia bar groups. I had readily agreed to make a presentation, and several weeks before the event, I'd sent in the materials I planned to use.

The event was to be a two-hour seminar with the first hour devoted to the ethics of marketing and the second devoted to a more-or-less open forum panel with me and two other attorneys leading the discussion.

I like these speaking opportunities for many reasons, but mostly because young lawyers are more entrepreneurial today than their counterparts were a decade ago, and they're open to new thinking.

But less than 24 hours before the scheduled event, I got that "Ben, we're very concerned" call from the president of the bar association. He called at 5:30 and told me he'd *just found out* I was speaking to the young lawyers the next afternoon. "I think some of your marketing materials are really not in line with our mission statement. As president, I can't just sit by and have you tell a room full of young lawyers that joining our voluntary bar and signing up for committees is not going to help them become good lawyers even though that's what you believe. We're a voluntary bar association, and we would *die* if no one volunteered."

Oh, brother. That's what you'll find yourself up against when you step off that traditional ladder. The elites won't like what you have to say. Mind you, this is a guy who hadn't read any of my books, attended any Great Legal Marketing event, or even shown up on a webinar.

By the way, if you're a young lawyer, know that he misquoted my position on "joining committees." I've never said that signing up for committees won't help lawyers become better lawyers. My position is that participating in bar events might make you a better lawyer if you ask the right questions, but that's not where you will find out how to get more clients. If building a business is your goal, I can give you a hundred better things to do than volunteer for a bar committee.

It was a strange call. Here's how I handled it:

1. I reminded him that his organization had invited me, not the other way around.

2. I reminded him that the event was less than 24 hours away and that he would have to scramble to find a replacement.

3. I told him I was his best advocate for young lawyers, but since he'd never seen me speak or read anything I'd written, he wouldn't know that.

He didn't disinvite me, though I certainly invited him to take that step. I was already thinking of the next great headline: "Banned by the local bar—what *they* don't want young lawyers to know about marketing."

BUSINESS OR PROFESSION?

Every so often, the blogosphere and listserves light up with the debate between those who say the practice of law is a profession and those who say it's a business. Usually, those advocating the profession side of the argument are really just arguing against marketing and advertising. They represent the "Do good work and they'll come" crowd.

At one time, I was a member of that crowd. When that's all you ever heard in law school and early on in the "profession," that's what you believe. When no one argues for or implores you to treat what you do as a business first and foremost, well, you don't know what you don't know.

Years ago, I was on the faculty of one of those "professionalism" courses in Virginia that we mandate all new lawyers attend. As you might imagine, my one-hour talk was a little different. The official title of my talk was something like, "The Conflicting Roles of Lawyer as Advocate and Businessperson." My talk was more aptly titled, "You Better Figure Out How to Get Business or There Will Be No Conflict to Worry About."

I covered everything from health and diet to (of all things) making money. My not-so-subliminal message was, "If you really follow everything else the folks on this stage are telling you today, you're going to be miserable and think that's just the way it is supposed to be."

I didn't last long on that circuit.

Last year, a poor sap here in Virginia turned in his license for good. His version of a Ponzi scheme involved creating fake pleadings to show his client all the work he was doing on a case that had long since been dismissed on procedural grounds. This went on for years. Who knows? Maybe he showed up for Professionalism Day after I'd been booted out. I'm just guessing he didn't have a system for running his business.

There's a reason I want you to become really good at marketing. It's because you are a hero. You can help people, and the world needs more of you. Truth is that folks who aren't good lawyers with integrity just don't seem to hang around me and my organization for long. There are many potential clients out there for whom you'd be the perfect lawyer, but if you aren't pushing every day to make their paths to you easy and obvious, they might find "Mr. Ponzi Schemer" who is starving and willing to do anything to get his next fee and keep the lights on. And if your potential clients go to him, shame on you and the rest of the profession for letting that happen.

Damn right we're running a business first.

Without a business, there's no profession to do.

CHAPTER 5

STUFF MARKETING VULTURES SAY, PART 1

I've long made fun of the marketing vultures, the folks selling advertising media such as websites, pay-per-click advertising, lead-generation services, TV and radio ads, and print advertising. They fill your email inbox with all those "We can help you with your website" messages. I like to bait them when they email me. Here's an actual unsolicited email from a vulture in late 2014:

> Hello,
>
> I run a few high authority private blog networks with relevant content to lawyers. These are high quality with zero footprint.
>
> I am reaching out to various SEO firms that work with lawyers to see if you are interested in renting out relevant links that you can use to boost your clients' sites. Please let me know if you are interested and I can send along more information.

This is currently the best way to create high quality sustainable backlinks to boost your clients' rankings.

Thanks,
Manu

My response was designed to "bait" him:

We are interested as long as this does not violate any Internet policies. Does this violate policy?

Ben Glass

His response to me:

Hello Ben,
Unfortunately, buying and selling links of any kind does go against Google's Webmaster Guidelines. However, they are just "guidelines" :)
This happens in practice every single day. In addition, I have set my links up in such a way that everything looks natural and there is no way Google's algorithm can find out.
Please let me know if you have any further questions.

Manu

Ah, yes. Let's try to fool Google!

There are no shortcuts. Zero. Anything that smells like a scam will eventually be caught by Google. They have hundreds of PhDs working on killing off this BS; don't find yourself in their crosshairs!

There are no shortcuts. Zero.

CHAPTER 6

STUFF MEDIA VULTURES SAY, PART 2

The information in this chapter is from court-filed and publicly available exhibits in a lawsuit by a law firm against a marketing company. The essence of the contract required the marketing company to conduct "link-building" and create "blog articles" to promote two law firm websites. I'll explain why even if the marketing company had done what the law firm alleges it was supposed to do under the contract, this was still money being pissed away. Good marketers understand the questions that must be asked of those selling the advertising.

The marketing contracts were executed in September 2011. One of the contracts was a one-year agreement at $1,750 per month ($21,000/year!) for link building. Under this agreement, the vendor was going to create a minimum of 2,000 unique, inbound links *each month* to the client's website. The links would be based on keywords and phrases that the vendor determined to be optimal for the law firm.

There was no mention or even recognition in the contracts of the importance of link *quality*. In fact, this contract specifically disclaimed that it could help the law firm website achieve any "increase in ranking results" or "improvements in search results." The first question a marketing-savvy lawyer would have asked was, "Why build these links at all?"

Later, the lawyers asked, "Where did you put these 24,000 links? Where can we go see them?" Response: "Sorry—trade secret." The second question that should have been asked *before* the contract was signed was, "How will we verify that you're doing what you are being paid to do?" So here we had lawyers signing a marketing services contract that, by its terms, professed to do *nothing* and, in practice, couldn't be verified.

The second contract was for "blog writing and social media marketing." The fee for this contract was $2,000 per month. The contract called for twenty *unique* blog posts each month. The vendor also agreed to begin "adding followers to the client's social media accounts."

This contract did provide some measurement of results. Specifically, the company would keep track of and report the number of Twitter followers, Facebook friends, LinkedIn connections, Facebook fans, unique visitors to the website, and calls on a unique phone number listed at the website. There were also provisions for tracking results all the way through leads and appointments and revenues. The agreement promised that over the twelve-month term of the agreement, the vendor would add a combined 3,600 to 4,800 new contacts, friends, followers, and first-level connections to the client's Facebook profile, Twitter accounts, and LinkedIn profile and groups.

This $45,000 for the year was for what we call "activity masquerading as accomplishment." Who cares how many people are your Facebook friends or connect to you on LinkedIn? You can't deposit digital friends in the bank. These shiny objects are attractive to lawyers because they show they are doing something cool, but they pale in comparison to genuine human relationships based on hard and authentic marketing, community connections, and having people truly evangelize for you. For $45,000, the firm could have hired a marketing assistant for a year! (See chapter 22, "So You're Thinking about Hiring a Marketing Director?")

The lawyers got fed up and sued, alleging all sorts of misrepresentations and throwing in a civil RICO claim for good measure.

The lawyers weren't so smart because even they didn't know the real problem with the deal. Sure, you can argue all day long about whether link building and article writing were effective tools for lawyer Internet marketing in late 2011, but the essential problem was that the website being promoted with these tools was very ordinary; it looked just like all those other boring lawyer websites. Consumers who actually got to the website found no good reason to interact with it, which is the whole point. Better to have taken all that money and invested it in fixing your website (see chapter 29, "Make Your Website Work for You"), creating reasons for visitors to interact with the site, and creating sophisticated follow-up sequences for those who did interact than to try to drive more people. It's like spending a bundle of money to get people to eat at a restaurant that gives people food poisoning.

That is precisely what the marketing vultures don't understand: marketing. Since they know that most lawyers don't understand it either, they get away with selling "purple pills."

Marketing vultures know very little about.... uh....Marketing.

CHAPTER 7

THAT 800-POUND GORILLA

Rejoice! The 800-pound gorillas really don't understand marketing either; they just spend money like it grows on trees.

Many lawyers get depressed when they see what the local 800-pound gorilla can do with a gargantuan marketing budget. You know whom I'm talking about: their faces are on every TV channel, city bus, and billboard for miles around. Some lawyers think those firms get all the cases. Fret no more. They don't. And from all I've seen, they don't know a whole lot about effective marketing either. Know this: around every Home Depot is a thriving mom and pop hardware store!

A particular lawyer marketing-centered lawsuit that went on for much of 2014 involved an antitrust claim arising out of bus advertising in Philadelphia and showed the ugly underworld of gorilla marketing.

Around every Home Depot is a thriving mom and pop hardware store!

In the lawsuit, the plaintiff law firm whined that it would be put out of business if it couldn't advertise on buses. Here's what the pleadings revealed they believed:

- They claimed consumers based their decisions for legal representation for small personal injury, Social Security disability, and workers' comp legal services primarily on *brand name recognition* and/or recall. (Some do, certainly, but this is not so for thousands of thriving solo and small law firms.)

- They claimed their business was *wholly* dependent on the ability of the firm to attract and ultimately sign engagement agreements with a high volume of individual clients. Law firms in the market for small personal injury, workers' compensation, and Social Security cases typically build their revenue by aggregating such clients in high volume. (This is a very stressful business model to choose, but it does suggest a marketing *message* for you: "We treat our clients individually, not as aggregate lumps of small bags of money.")

- They claimed that if a potential client wasn't exposed to the name of a firm on a routine, consistent, and repetitive basis, that client wouldn't know to call the firm's phone number. (This just isn't true anywhere the Internet exists.)

- They said that the way to get the biggest "bang for the buck" (their terms) was to advertise legal services through mass reach outlets using constant messaging and saturation advertising. (Again, not for thousands of lawyers who understand the type of marketing we teach.)

- They insisted that without mass advertising, law firms practicing in these areas were *unable to compete effectively and efficiently.* (Sad.)

- They wrote, "The most effective and, therefore most coveted, mass reach, constant messaging, saturation advertisements that provide the greatest return for the cost spent are those: (1) placed on the exterior of buses; (2) aired on radio in prime time slots such as rush hour and during traffic updates; and (3) displayed inside arenas where sporting and concert events are regularly held." (Really? You go to a basketball game and you text your lawyer?)

- They claimed these three forms of advertising were far more effective than other forms such as television, the Internet, and the Yellow Pages. (They're probably correct about the Yellow Pages.)

- They said, "There is no economically viable substitute for bus exterior advertising, and none of the available advertising alternatives are as effective and efficient because they cannot achieve the same consumer recognition that bus exterior advertising does without a cost-prohibitive amount of money."

- They said the Internet wasn't as effective or as efficient a form of advertising as bus exteriors because the sheer volume of information available on the Internet makes it virtually impossible for one law firm to distinguish itself from others in a particular market. (This is true if your web team doesn't know what it's doing.)

- They whined, "Consumers are often quick to conclude that a law firm that no longer advertises on bus exteriors may no longer be in existence." (Wow!)

Here's how smart solo and small-firm lawyers think: let the big firms spend their money that way while we work on ways to get more out of every dollar and every hour we spend on marketing.

Next time you see a lawyer running a bus ad, thank him for not directing that dollar toward effective marketing!

In the following few chapters, I'll spill some ink on the importance of how you think about things—things such as marketing, the practice of law, and your life itself.

Feel free to skip this section if you want and go straight into the marketing strategies, but I urge you to stick around and read this part first.

In my view, the insider secret about marketing is that what goes on inside your head is far more important than the words you put on paper, the ads you run on TV, or whether your website features a gavel or a book. Marketing techniques and tools are important, no doubt, but getting your head on straight is a condition precedent to success.

CHAPTER 8

WHAT DO YOU THINK ABOUT? IDEAS, THINGS, OR PEOPLE?

Long ago, I heard the axiom, "Big people talk about ideas, average people talk about things, and little people talk about other people." I think I may have seen it in one of those *Habits of the Super Successful* books.

I believe this is true when it comes to life, and it's certainly true when it comes to marketing. I find that most of the successful attorneys I work with spend time thinking about, coming up with, and working on the big ideas: Whom do I want to see walking through the door of my perfect practice? What kind of marketing message would attract those perfect clients? What type of experience will those people have as they walk through my marketing processes? Once they become clients, how will they feel as our team helps them solve their legal problems?

Such lawyers are constantly searching for ideas. They're curious about how other successful business owners (and not just lawyers) market, how they learned about marketing, and whom they read on the topic of marketing (in whatever business they are in). They never end their marketing and business education—they test ideas against reality and leave guesswork and hunches to the average lawyer.

"Big people talk about ideas, average people talk about things, and little people talk about other people."

Most lawyers don't think that way at all. They worry about what web company is best, which vulture they should buy leads from, what their logos look like, and whether they should be advertising on a closed-circuit TV at fitness centers. Those are *things*, which are important, but they are nowhere near as important as *ideas*. If things are the first thing you think about when it comes to marketing and ideas come after that, you have it backwards.

Some lawyers have a "scarcity" mentality. They think that if Lawyer Jones gets a client, there are no more clients for them. These people spend little time thinking about ideas or things; they just self-commiserate and invite others to join in their whine parties.

The "ideas first and things second" thinking extends far beyond marketing, of course. It's actually a good lesson for life. I encourage you to carve out some time to think deeply about what you think about most. How's your brain wired? It is time for a rewiring?

CHAPTER 9

THE SECRET IS THE "MENTAL" THING

During the 2014 GLM National Summit, one attendee came up to me at the end of the first day with a complaint: "This was all about mind-set. I'm looking for the newest version of the secret sauce." He was wrong about what we had talked about that day (and he had come in late, beer in hand, to the marketing expert roundtables we held after dinner, at which some of our top members answered every question posed to them), but I offered him our immediate, on-the-spot refund. He declined. We didn't see him much on day two, either. Oh, well.

I remembered that conversation when my son David pointed out an article in the *Wall Street Journal*. He was 17 at the time; we had adopted him from China when he was 12. He runs track and cross country. We read the *Wall Street Journal* every morning. David has many questions about politics, international relations, and the news in general.

The article in the *Journal* was about a high school cross-country team in New York that consistently produced teams that ran in the national cross-country championships. (Cross ntry is a team sport; in a race, the winner gets one point, second place two, and so on. The teams are comprised of seven runners each. The team with the lowest point total wins; thus, you must have a bunch of good runners, not just one or two stars, to win a race.) This school has won nine national titles (boys and girls) in nine years. What was incredible was that it was a public school drawing students from within its boundaries.

As the article pointed out, the secret sauce was not a top-secret training program that no one else knew about. Quoting from a *Runner's World* writer, the *Journal* wrote that the secret was the mental thing. For this team, the mental thing combined a study of philosophy; disciplined eating, sleeping, and training; and a "devotion to one's principles." The team adopted a different way of thinking about the world around its members and bought into the reason they existed as a team. The Fayetteville-Manlius (Syracuse, NY) cross-country team had a set of unwavering values that the leader coached from and insisted on, and he (likely) dismissed those unable to comply with them.

You can decide that mind-set doesn't matter, but I challenge you to show me an organization that's consistently successful but pays no attention to the mind-set thing.

CHAPTER 10

WHAT'S YOUR "WHY"?

When I first started learning about marketing, I discovered the concept of the unique selling proposition, or USP. As my friend, marketing and business-building genius Dan Kennedy, says, a USP is the "reason why someone would choose to do business with you over all other choices, including the choice to do nothing."

As I developed marketing programs for my law firm, I modified the concept of USP a bit. I asked myself, *Why would a potential client reach out and begin a conversation with me rather than all the other choices he has, including the choice to do nothing or even attempt to handle his legal situation on his own?*

The most advanced lawyer marketers know that coming up with a USP for a law firm is difficult. It can't be reduced to a pithy slogan or catchy tagline; it's real. And it must cause action on the part of the prospect.

Understanding your "why" is critical to your success. Understanding your why leads you to understand who your perfect client is. Understanding who your perfect client is enables you to create marketing messages just for him. Most lawyer marketing messages shout, "We are for everyone and everyone's for us." Not too differentiating, is it?

But what is this "why"? What does that really mean? Again, it's neither slogan nor tagline; it's the answer to the question, "What would your community lose if your practice ceased to exist?" If your answer is "Not much" or even "I'm not sure" or worse, "Nothing," you have to give serious thought to changing that thinking in your mind and in your community's mind. It can't be "We care" or "We're aggressive" or "We've been around 415 years."

"What would your community lose if your practice ceased to exist?"

If these are your answers, however, know that you can turn things around. At BenGlassLaw, our "why" is *helping people make great decisions about their legal situations.* We do this by being willing to provide more information, from self-help for those who want to handle their cases alone, to detailed deposition preparation packages complete with a CD that we created, to written settlement evaluations in *every case* so our clients and prospects are empowered. Everything we do, every ad we run, every message we communicate in person with clients and prospects are centered around this "why."

A deep dive now into what it means for a law firm to have a "why" and what that might be for you is beyond the scope

of this book. A book you should read right after
Beyond Entrepreneurship by James Collins. Grab i
it. It's old, but I discovered it in doing some res
how good ideas become great entrepreneurial successes.
This is the book Collins published nine years before his epic
Good to Great. It's a treasure, and Amazon has it. After you
read that, try *Scaling Up*, by Verne Harnish.

CHAPTER 11

NO NEED FOR *THAT* CONVERSATION

When a potential new client wants to make sure you know he's interviewing other attorneys (often to get a fee reduction or some other consideration from you), he'll ask, "What makes you different? Why should I hire you?"

How do you respond?

I was so proud to hear my newest associate answering that question on the phone as I walked down the hall one day. He said, "You know, sir, it doesn't exactly work that way here. We're very busy. Most people I talk to have read Mr. Glass's consumer books on the law, and the only question is whether we're going to accept your case or not. So the question we have is whether your case *qualifies* for our representation."

If you're being asked to *sell me on you*, that's a clue you're not differentiating yourself in your marketing. When you walk into the room to meet potential clients for the first time, they ought to be thunderstruck by the opportunity to finally get to meet you in person. You shouldn't be easy to get to, and you shouldn't ever be answering the "How are you different?" question. If they have to ask that, you haven't done your marketing correctly or they haven't paid attention to it. If it's the latter, I can almost guarantee they won't be good clients for you. You shouldn't be the one having to do the convincing at that first meeting. If you are, think about how hard it's going to be for them to take your advice in a difficult case later!

> **When you walk into the room to meet potential clients for the first time, they ought to be thunderstruck by the opportunity to finally get to meet you in person.**

CHAPTER 12

DEVELOPING A "GET IT ALL DONE" MIND-SET

For me, getting an extraordinary amount of work accomplished comes down to a couple of key mind-set points:

- A determination that what I do is for the good morally. (I'm not just talking about it being "morally good" to help people. I'm talking about it being morally good to pursue what you want in life for your own happiness.)

- A clear idea of where my ships are heading based on what I believe to be in my and my family's best interest. This is goal setting.

- A decision to incorporate as many business systems into my law practice as possible.

- A ruthless (sometimes even mean) protection of my time from time vampires.

• A determination that if you're not a superstar, you can't be on my team even if you were considered a superstar someplace else.

• A commitment when communicating with employees to teaching not only *how* we do something but also *why* we do it so they can be empowered to make great decisions on their own.

By the way, I dive deep into these philosophies on the CD that comes with this book. If you purchased the eBook version or want to download it, go to RenegadeLawyerBonus.com and type "vulture" in the space where it asks for a code.

If you're not a superstar, you can't be on my team.

CHAPTER 13

WHO SAYS YOU HAVE TO SERVE THE CLIENT?

I know this is a controversial topic, but hear me out. I often hear lawyers at "regular" lawyer seminars talk about "serving the client." You'll hear people say they went to law school to "serve others." When my son graduated from law school, former justice of the United States Supreme Court Sandra Day O'Connor told the graduates they must "serve a new master." Sadly, I've heard some lawyers tell tales of marching straight to the poorhouse based on a fundamental misunderstanding of what serving the client means in real life.

I'm a huge fan of John Allison, who built BB&T Bank. Finding BB&T's principles on the Internet is well worth the time. The book *I Am John Galt* has an excellent chapter on Allison's mindset. Even if you're not, as I am, an Ayn Rand fan, this book is worth reading. Allison, a Christian, built BB&T on Rand's philosophy of "objectivism." Rand was an atheist. (Interesting to read how Allison dealt with that.)

Allison prided himself on "teaching BB&T employees 'how to think.'" He believed that all his employees needed

43

to be "self-guided missiles" and that to achieve that, they had to be superbly trained. In Allison's mind, the goal of training his employees well was *not* to serve clients; the goal was to create superior long-term results for the owners, the shareholders, of BB&T. The owners, he said, provided the capital (thus taking on risk), so they had the right to receive economic rewards for that risk.

Whether or not you are the owner of your firm, this applies to you. The firm you own or work for must make a profit *before* it provides legal services to anyone.

But what about the "serving clients" part? Don't you have to serve them? Must your doors be open to everyone? Doesn't that come first? Nope. Client satisfaction, Allison says, is an essential means to the goal of wealth creation for the owner. You serve clients well because that's how you make money. You don't serve in the self-sacrificial way of putting their interests above yours just because they need you and your talents.

Go back and read that last line carefully. You do good work because this is what you are paid to do, and the reason you're running a law practice is to make money.

If you have no money, you have no business. If you have no business, you have no ability to serve anyone, deserving or not. That's an important distinction in my view; it's important because it helps with decision making. How many files do you have right now in your office that are sucking the lifeblood out of your firm? Why are they there?

To some, this sounds harsh—even cruel—and contrary to everything they've thought about the profession. I suggest that developing a solid philosophy and living by its principles is the only way to live and run a business. Every

time I go against my own philosophy (and beli
happens), I make a mistake.

The firm you own or work for must make a profit *before* it provides legal services to anyone.

You need rules. We have rules in our office for case nonacceptance—too close to the statute of limitations, another lawyer handled it even a little bit, the case has already been filed, the case was not accepted because of philosophical differences about the type of case, and so on. We even have rules about (stereo)types of people we simply won't accept no matter how good their cases sound!

Cruel. Harsh. But necessary for survival. And very practical.

Reriek
out

CHAPTER 14

TASTES JUST LIKE HEART-RATE TRAINING

When you start learning about marketing, the subject can be overwhelming. I understand that keeping fit is one of the secrets to long life, but keeping up with the science of fitness can be overwhelming.

I am fifty-seven. I do all my aerobic training with heart-rate monitoring, and my "bible" is *Heart Rate Training* by Roy Benson and Declan Connolly. Here's a cool paragraph extolling the benefits of slow but steady training. Referring to a workout that seems too simple, slow, and short to be of any benefit, the authors say:

> This 20 minute period may seem too short, and with the intensity so low, you may think that it is too easy. You may wonder whether you'll ever get in shape at this rate. But hold on. This is a very delicate period of adaptation. Your muscular system will get stronger rather quickly thanks to its good blood supply and may give you the impression that you're ready for bigger and better workouts ... your engine will start adding horsepower.

This is exactly what we're doing with our marketing. You can't accomplish it all at once, particularly if you've never thought much about marketing before, but you can achieve long-lasting marketing "fitness" if you do something proactive every day. While our competition sleeps in, we're already on the road. It may seem slow, and it can certainly be boring. We may see setbacks (for instance, Google's never-ending algorithm changes can throw even the most conscientious marketer for a loop). But we're building collateral circulation. Our engines are developing more horsepower. It's virtually impossible to fail to succeed if we put on our shoes and get out there. One day, we wake up, look at our new case stats, and say, "Gee, how did we get there? Oh, yeah. One step at a time. Every day. Even when it rains or the temps topped 90."

Here's a practice Dan Kennedy taught me: every day, make sure you do at least one thing to fill the pipeline.

It's virtually impossible to fail to succeed if we put on our shoes and get out there.

CHAPTER 15

DON'T LET SYSTEMS SCARE YOU

I'm a huge Michael Gerber fan. Yes, that Michael Gerber, the bestselling author and renowned small business evolutionary. Michael Gerber, creator of the E-Myth series of books for entrepreneurs. Gerber's primary thesis is that you should always be building systems in your business that would permit the business to be franchised and then run by others.

Gerber and I even created a product for lawyers about systematizing marketing. When we launched that product, we received feedback. While my own MasterMind members ate it up, some nonmembers expressed surprise at my teaming up with Michal Gerber, the "systems guy." Typical of the response: "McDonald's was built on systems. Teenagers can run it. My law practice is different. I give individualized care and can't imagine 'building my practice in order to franchise it.' That's not the practice of law."

Baloney! Think about it. Track what you and your staff do all week. I'm betting that upward of 95 percent of what happens in your practice is repeated each week and some

51

s repeated every day. And most of it is repeated by people other than you.

Why would anyone be afraid to put into place processes that guarantee when something is repeated in your office, it's repeated to your high standards? Why are you involved in much of anything that you could model and then have repeated by others in your firm? Creating a system that even a teenager could run (I'm just a teeny-weeny bit away from kidding about the teenager part—the average age in my office is 23) frees you to do what your client paid you to do: be the chief strategist who can direct the solving of the client's problem. That's your primary job. Your second most important job is to create those systems.

I used to think that clients actually wanted and expected me to be familiar with all parts of their cases at all times. That was a lot for me to keep up with; I run a busy practice. Here's the exact conversation that goes on during a meeting where a fee agreement is being signed:

> Okay, here's how this works. I'm the chief strategist and trial lawyer on your case, but there are hundreds of things that go on in a case that don't really involve me directly. I'm responsible, of course, but I've hired and trained a team of folks who will do these things for you and me in the case. So, Sally and Bill, their job is to go out and work with you to track down all the important data in your case. Suzie's job is to manage all that data as it comes in, and together, they bring to my attention any problems or issues. From time to time, when they report to

RENEGADE LAWYER MARKETING

me that issues have cropped up, that's when I get involved. We have great systems for getting this done. If you ever feel the need to talk directly to me, just let us know and we'll set that up.

Once all that data is in, I work with you to arrive at a settlement strategy. If that doesn't result in a settlement, we're into litigation. Here's the litigation team, and here's what they do, and here are the systems for making sure that what they will do will all get done to my very high standards. And if that doesn't work, I'm your trial lawyer on the case.

Not only are they not disappointed that I'm not involved in every detail and know about the status of their entire case every single day, they also love the fact that my team has their backs. For real.

Next up, Marketing. I'll take you through the basics of marketing. I'll start out with A One-Chapter Marketing Bible (that's the title of the chapter) that will give you a broad overview. Subsequent chapters will deal with such matters to how to design your marketing materials around your avatar client and how to launch your marketing campaign. I'll be giving you a good number of steps to follow, but they all lead to a pot of gold.

CHAPTER 16

A ONE-CHAPTER MARKETING BIBLE

Create and master these five systems for a happier, more lucrative practice. Don't worry if you see some concepts mentioned here that you don't understand, as we will dig in deep in future chapters. You will also find examples in chapter 23 .

1. **A Client-Attraction System**

    Most lawyers have one call to action: "Call me now!" You need to give people an alternate reason to contact you because some aren't yet ready to make an appointment even though they have a problem you could solve.

    You need an information lead magnet, typically, a print book you also make available in an e-book format. If you don't have one, start putting out a free report or white paper. You will find some examples in chapter 23. The best marketers have many, one for each point on the "moving parade of interest" a potential client might have. You then develop collateral marketing material that gives people a reason to be attracted to you and your book or paper because it's different and interesting. That system tracks everything.

2. **A Client-Conversion System**

Many lawyers don't need to invest more money in getting more leads—they need to fix their existing conversion system to convert the leads they're receiving into actual clients. You must create training and scripts for the folks answering the calls, or if the response mechanism is to fill out a web form, then what the potential client sees on a landing page after he hits "send" must be interesting, informative, and relevant to what he just asked for. You need to develop your version of a "shock and awe" package, an information package that "shows up like no one else's."[1]* Finally, you need an automated follow-up system for unconverted leads.

3. **A System for Collecting Testimonials, Especially for the Online Consumer Rating Sites such as Google and Avvo**

Like it or not, your prospects are checking you out by reviewing online lawyer rating information. Your hating it doesn't mean they won't do it. Right

---

1 *My friend Dan Kennedy invented the term "shock and awe package," and when he spoke for us at the National Summit, he introduced the term "showing up like no one else." If you've never listened to that one-of-a-kind presentation Dan did for us; fax a request on your law firm letterhead to 877-576-6752. As an unadvertised reward for actually reading this book, I'll send you the two-disc set as a bonus!

now, BenGlassLaw has more favorable consumer ratings and lawyer endorsements on Avvo than any other law firm in Virginia, and we're using that fact in our marketing. We have more Google reviews than any other lawyer who shows up on Google when you search for a personal injury lawyer in our area. That's not random. We have a system that encourages consumers to tell others about us, and we make it easy for them to do so.

Most important, we don't wait until the end of the case to get them to write about us. Our system is run by Infusionsoft. I have joint ventured with that company to create a software module that incorporates the Great Legal Marketing philosophy. (You can get more information at GLMLovesInfusionsoft.com.)

4. **A System for Creating and Encouraging Evangelists**
What others say about you is far more powerful than anything you could say about yourself. We all have our "fans"—those people who have requested information from us and who now get marketing from us. They get specific marketing when they are prospects who have raised their hands, and they get a mailed monthly newsletter as long as they're still living in our market area. That's your basic system. The "advanced" evangelist system recognizes that a segment of your herd really does love you and will go out of their way to tell your story, distribute your books, and even look for opportunities to refer.

They get more marketing from us, such as an expensive magazine and random cool stuff such as luggage tags and cell phone chargers. Your mavens can get invited to client appreciation dinners. (Again, ask my MasterMind members Mark and Alexis Breyer, BreyerLaw.com, about this, and go to Women's Night Out, hosted by Kristen Hofheimer, VirginiaDivorceAttorney.com) The point is that you need to know who your top referral sources are, and they need to know you're paying attention to them.

What others say about you is far more powerful than anything you could say about yourself.

---

5. A Specific System for Increasing Referrals from Other Professionals and Business Owners

Getting referrals from other respected "herd" leaders is huge. You want this to be an orchestrated, not a random, process. The single best way to get such referrals is to look around your community, find people who could be referring clients to you, and ask yourself, *What can I do for these people or businesses first?*

The easiest way to start this process is to write about them in your monthly newsletter or ask them to consider contributing an article. The advanced strategy is to invite them to your video studio for interviews that promote *them,* not you. To see some examples of how we have done this at BenGlassLaw, go to CharityVideoSamples.com.

CHAPTER 17

WHAT YOU CAN LEARN FROM MY ATTORNEY MASTERMIND GROUP

This marketing formula doesn't change even when you get really good at marketing. I run an area-exclusive attorney MasterMind Group that meets in person for two days, three times a year. During these confidential meetings, member firms take turns in the hot seat to talk about what's working and what's not and to ask the others in the group for input on both. We distribute and ooh and aah over lots of marketing materials, including newsletters, books, magazines, bags, and other "branded" goodies. More important, we take deep dives into each other's practices.

After one of the 2014 meetings, as I was driving a couple of members to the airport, Charter MasterMind member Chuck Boyk (Toledo, CharlesBoykLaw.com) made a very interesting comment.

> You know, it's amazing. We've been doing this for years. We've seen a ton of marketing ideas. Some have come and disappeared as valuable

tools. The Internet is getting to be more difficult for everyone. TV and radio are very fractured. It's just interesting that we keep coming back to the basics ... the things that worked then and still work now.

He's right. We had presentations from 21 law firms. They were, in large part, in different practice areas (including personal injury, family, workers' comp, bankruptcy, franchise law, Social Security disability, defense of health professionals in front of licensing boards, and class action among them), and they were spread across the four corners of the country and Canada. Some are still reporting enormous ROI with the Yellow Pages!

Most of the MasterMind members have been a part of that group for over seven years, and each of these very successful firms has tried hundreds and hundreds of marketing ideas over the years; none was using any sort of unusual or unique marketing. Most report that a majority of their income comes not from advertising for new clients, per se, but from marketing through their herds or "tribes." In other words, the majority of their income comes from some sort of referral process.

While the individual marketing pieces and strategies we discussed are confidential to the group (and shared not only at meetings, but also on a private listserve), the list of principles you'd run across in these presentations includes the following:

1. They get really good at a handful of marketing techniques or strategies, and they execute them

flawlessly. Rather than creating new ads or other marketing pieces, they continually refine what they're already doing to make what they have even better. This includes making sure their follow-up campaigns are as personalized and as deep as they can be.

2. They print and mail newsletters. Every month. The newsletters are dense with interesting copy, not just legal articles. (More about this in chapter 28, "You Need an Interesting Newsletter" chapter.)

3. They have excellent websites, but they are *decreasing* the amount of content they're creating for their sites. That's right, decreasing it. Instead, they're improving the quality of the content they already have on their sites. They're students of copywriting.

4. They work on their referral sources. At our meetings, we have seen the inside of Chuck Boyk's (CharlesBoyk-Law.com) referral marketing system, and it's exhausting, but the result is that everyone in Toledo knows him. One of his referral campaigns made him the lead news item on local TV over and over, week after week, during the summer. (Read that again. That's not a typo.).

Phoenix member **Mark Breyer** (BreyerLaw.com) put it this way: one person who knows you is more valuable than a hundred who know your name. (This is why it's much more important to develop authentic relationships than to pay some marketing vulture to get Facebook "likes.")

Several, including national franchise expert **Charles Internicola,** (FranchiseLawSolutions.com) have started local mastermind groups and invite referral sources who "get it" to share business growth practices in monthly meetings. These are not "You refer to me and I'll refer to you" meetings; rather, these are "What do you know about client or customer acquisition that I may be able use in my law firm" type meetings.

5. They know their mavens—their top referral sources—and they treat them better than they do the rest. (All 100 percent within ethical guidelines—I'm not talking about payola here!)

6. They train all their employees to answer the phones right, and they continually monitor to make sure this happens. They don't let their marketing dollars get burned up by a bad telephone answering experience.

7. They continually *build equity* in their firms by bringing the marketing in house. Just about everyone has at least one "marketing assistant" who is "GLM trained." In fact, many of the marketing assistants attend the meetings with us. Some even have in-house videographers, SEO/webmasters, and graphic artists.

CHAPTER 18

GET BETTER AT MARKETING—IT'S YOUR DUTY

You don't need to be a pioneer to get better at marketing your firm, but you do need to know whom to listen to, and it helps to be a renegade with ambition.

— In every market in America, you can find solo and small firms that are rocking it with their marketing but not spending a ton of money to do so. These lawyers stand out, they make a great living, and they enjoy the practice of law. You don't have to reinvent the wheel to achieve the same for yourself. The strategies and tactics of successful solo and small firms can be modeled even by big firms, though this is rare. They are not as nimble as you are.

Modeling those who are successful at marketing their small firms is key. What are they doing different than you? How do they *think* about marketing in a way that allows them to compete with the 800-pound gorillas in their markets?

One thing is very clear: doing what the majority does results in getting what the majority gets—average results. You're made for more than average. Be a renegade. Think differently. Yes, think outside the box.

While many lawyers are shy about being considered good at marketing, the smartest lawyers are not only comfortable with the idea, they also embrace effective marketing as a part of their *obligation* as lawyers.

Let me ask you a few questions. Are you a good lawyer? Do you deliver quality services? Are you ethical? Do you and your staff put the client first and make him feel great about having hired you? Do you believe that right now someone in your locale is looking for a lawyer and that you'd be the perfect lawyer to solve his legal problem? Do you think that person might be the perfect client for you—someone who has a problem you can solve and who will respect you and your staff and pay his bill (or generate a contingent fee)?

If your answers are all yesses, why would you not try to get your message out to that person and prevent him from walking into the firm down the street that wouldn't be as good for him as your firm would be? That's a big part of what we're supposed to be doing as lawyers, isn't it? Getting the right people to the right lawyer so everyone with a legitimate need for legal services can actually access those services. I argue that this is your *duty*.

Boring, dull, and way-too-general lawyer advertising and marketing doesn't get the right people to the right lawyers, and it won't attract the right people to you except by blind luck.

And blind luck is not a good business plan.

Blind luck is not a good business plan.

CHAPTER 19

GOOD MARKETING: DESIGN WHAT YOU WANT YOUR LIFE TO LOOK LIKE

What a strange title for a chapter on marketing, but without what you want for your life, there can be no focus to your marketing. Might as well just hand the money over blindfolded.

For the first 12 years of my professional practice life, I worked as an associate and then as a partner at a firm that primarily did insurance defense work. I really didn't have much control over anything, and none of the folks I hung out with (other insurance defense attorneys), ever said anything about my controlling things. Most of what I heard was about how lousy the work was, how much fighting these lawyers did with the insurance companies who paid their bills, and how miserable it made their families. That's the way it was in our practice. All that and plenty of daily chaos ,as well! We had virtually no systems in place for anything except getting our bills out the door.

When that's all you hear, your thoughts become your reality. When Sandi complained about my being away or working late or on weekends, I told her she and the kids *just needed to understand.*

Your thoughts become your reality.

When I left that firm to start my own practice, I thought things would be different because I'd be in charge and my practice wasn't going to be so chaotic. I'd start to read books such as *Think and Grow Rich* or *7 Habits of Highly Effective People,* but I'd put them aside because I'd convince myself that self-determination wasn't possible for a law practice. A thought nagged me: *How can I choose the practice and life I want when the flow of new clients is so random?* Besides, none of the other lawyers I was hanging out with seemed to be living self-determined lives, either.

I still struggle from time to time with a belief system that tells me, *I can design my life.* Sure, life throws you curveballs, but today, by and large, I do craft my own existence. And that existence I've created for my family, my firm, and my clients is fed by a marketing system that works.

CHAPTER 20

HOW HARD IS THIS, REALLY?

How much do you really need to know to effectively market your firm? Marketing strategies abound; you'll find *gurus* on every corner. So how much do you really need to know to make significant changes in your life?

Relax. You don't need to become an *uber* expert in the intricacies of search engine optimization, blogging, pay-per-click advertising, or "retargeting" with banner ads. Since most lawyer advertising is pretty crappy, you actually just need to be just a little better than your local competition. You can develop a fun, successful, and profitable practice without spending all, or even most, of your time marketing. But you do need to understand the essentials, and you must have a way to develop and deploy strategies, just as you need to understand your area of law and how to get work done.

At the very least, you should have a good understanding of:

1. How to create a good marketing message that will provoke both those ready to hire a lawyer

and those who aren't quite ready to move forward to contact you. You can choose to use the same message everyone else uses ("Free Consultation," "No Fee if No Recovery," "Lowest Price"), but that makes no sense; doing what the crowd does won't get you very far unless you can outspend them.

Since most lawyer advertising is pretty crappy, you actually just need to be just a little better than your local competition.

Our solo and small-firm members learn how to create messages that, in addition to offering an appointment, generally contain some form of this message: "Raise your hand and get your free information *before* you make a move." That free information is usually a book, though it could also be an informative video. You then make a trade: contact information from them in exchange for your book or access to your video.

2. **How important having a book is.** I talk about the importance of your writing a book in detail in chapter 23. Think about what's going on as you read this book. Hopefully, what you are thinking is, *Ben Glass knows more about marketing than I do. I need to explore what he's doing. How can I get more involved?* The publisher of this book, Word Association, is

the world's leading publisher of lawyer-authored consumer books on the law. They get what we do and would be happy to help you become a published authority in your practice area.

3. **How best to use Internet marketing.** You can improve the chances you'll be found by potential clients and have prospects stick around on your site long enough to find out that what you offer is interesting, but you need to understand the basics. Leaving Internet marketing entirely up to the folks selling you such services is like not asking your doctor anything when she says, "Let's go have surgery." We dig deeper on this in chapter 29.

4. **How to manage a marketing database.** You need to have a database and know how to use it so you can stay in constant, interesting communication with prospects and clients alike. A simple email autoresponder is not robust enough! Using your general case-management software for marketing won't work either.

5. **How valuable complexity is.** Buying TV time? Revamping your website? Running a print ad? Most lawyers stop thinking once an ad is completed, but good marketers think about the next step. What do they want responders to do? What will the irresistible call to action be? How will they track it? What will the secondary call to action be? What happens to

the people who *almost* picked up the phone to call them but didn't?

Okay, true confession: marketing a law practice well is not easy. If it were, everyone would be good at it. I get it; you're busy. You didn't go to law school to learn to be a marketer, but you can't ignore the importance of marketing any more than you can avoid learning something about the income tax system. The better you get at managing your marketing as well as your taxes, the more money you will make and keep!

CHAPTER 21

MARKETING TO YOUR AVATAR CLIENTS

You can't create effective marketing without deciding whom you want to see walking through your office door as a result of that marketing. You'd probably agree that you like certain clients but that others drive you crazy. I have a big message for you: you don't have to take on Mr. Crazy or Mrs. Time Suck anymore.

I'm primarily a personal injury attorney. I used to think there were no "demographics," so to speak, when it came to car-accident cases. After all, you get hit, you get hit. The dude who was driving the truck that hit you didn't check out your age, height, or income status before he tweeted or reached down for another can of Red Bull, did he? And I also used to think that with so much competition for personal injury cases, how could I afford to be picky? Doesn't the little case today mean the big case of tomorrow?

Here's what I want you to do right now: first step, write down the characteristics of your avatar client. (And be sure to involve your staff in the discussion. After all, they'll be the ones primarily dealing with these folks.) For my personal injury clients, some go almost automatically on my "no" list—those with low property damage, prior lawsuits, prior attorney working on the case, and so on. I'm sure you and your staff could come up with that list for your practice area as well. Having internal rules about case acceptance helps drive the focus of the marketing and makes case acceptance decision making easier.

Second step, list your current clients who cause bile to rise up your esophagus whenever you hear they're on the phone. Figure out what it is about them that causes that reaction in you, and figure out how they got past your "no" sign. That's an important step in creating filters that will keep people like that out of your practice in the future. (And if in doing this exercise you realize there are some clients you should fire tomorrow, do it!)

I hear your objection: "I have to take these cases to keep the lights on. These are my bread-and-butter cases!" I thought the same way at one time, but after hearing how other (more-successful) attorneys had changed their criteria and eliminated such clients from their practices (and thus from their lives and nightmares) even before they could afford to, I decided to change my practice. Once I figured that out, we started turning away even big cases where a potential client just didn't fit our criteria.

A few years ago, my MasterMind members Mark and Alexis Breyer (BreyerLaw.com) made a decision to absolutely not take any more soft-tissue cases. These are folks who do a lot of advertising and, at the time, their advertising attracted many soft-tissue cases. The decision to cut out those types of cases caused a lot of anxiety and fear.

They asked themselves, *Will this really make sense for us?* In 2014, they had to build a new building, tripling their space!

Another member decided to charge an initial consultation fee of $500 for DUI cases. This is almost unheard of in a practice area that, if you listen to the crowd, tends to be price sensitive. Today, he makes more than six figures just on the DUI cases he refers out!

Like Apple's founder, Steve Jobs, you create your own reality. This is part of creating your perfect life: do it on paper first and just start. Screw waiting for perfect timing. I promise you that once you get tough and turn away a couple of folks who just don't cut it for you, you'll get addicted to it. You and your staff will high five each other going forward.

Here's a big key: take the huge amount of time you just saved by not accepting those who don't perfectly meet your criteria and invest that time in the creation of another marketing piece that will attract the clients you want.

As they used to say in the old Alka-Seltzer commercial, "Try it, you'll like it."

You create your own reality.

So those are the marketing basics. Now for the part you probably invested in this book for. What I'll do next is take you through the process of creating a more-detailed marketing program. I'll let Charley Mann, our chief marketing officer, help you decide if you should hire a marketing officer in the next chapter. Then, I'll list the steps you should take to create your own campaign and take you through how to actually launch your campaign.

CHAPTER 22

SO YOU'RE THINKING ABOUT HIRING A MARKETING DIRECTOR?

(Charley Mann, Chief Marketing Officer of Great Legal Marketing)

I hear the following question all the time: "*When* should I hire a marketing director or assistant?" I'll go ahead and shortcut to the answer for you: Now. Or, at the very least, as soon as you can. Honestly, someone in your office focusing on marketing will be a major multiplier of your efforts. You've still got cases to handle and appointments to attend. Marketing-focused employees have one responsibility: making sure you have more appointments to attend and cases to handle. They should stay busy keeping you busy. When done right, the position doesn't just pay for itself. It has a significant return on investment that grows with time.

I will now tell you that the "when" question is second in quantity only to "*How* do I hire a marketing director/ assistant (who won't suck)?"

The reason I get asked this question all the time is because of the unique position in which I sit and how I got to this point—and because I now do all the hiring for BenGlassLaw and Great Legal Marketing. The best way I can teach you about how to hire a marketing assistant is for me to just tell my own story.

(Note: I'm going to use the word *assistant* throughout this story because that's where my journey began. You should, however, feel free to mentally substitute in the word "director" if that is what you are looking for in your practice.)

Here's the first things you need to know: I was not a marketing major, and I don't have an MBA. I don't even have a communications degree or business degree. I was, in fact, a theater major in college (with a minor in English, not that you asked). In my last year of college, I started a fantasy football podcast and website, the name of which escapes me at this moment but likely involved a pun on my last name. I also wrote for the sports website Bleacher Report, and I was the Featured Columnist for the Denver Broncos.

This is all to say that I was *not* hired for looks-good-on-paper reasons, though starting a website from scratch was a plus, as was being able to hit editorial deadlines. I was hired for my enthusiasm and an intense interest in learning. I got my job only because Ben decided to put on Craigslist a job ad unlike any other I'd read; he had designed it to both attract and repel applicants. Ben was taking his marketing knowledge and applying it to the hiring process. He was on the search for his ideal team members. The job listing contained information like this:

- We're looking for college students or recent graduates who would be interested in learning how to succeed at Internet marketing. We have a big video project that will involve figuring out how to use a new piece of software and creating brand-new videos to upload online.

- If your mom and dad had to check to make sure you did your homework even when you were in college, this is not going to be the job for you.

- We want to work with ambitious, hard-working people. We want to show you how you can take what you learn at this job and be even more successful wherever you go next.

- We think you will be successful at this job if you have some experience blogging (WordPress, Blogger, etc.), you've created basic videos, and you have a basic understanding of search engine optimization (SEO).

I'm going to share a secret right here, right now, that I haven't revealed before. Don't tell Ben about this part. I had no clue what "search engine optimization" was when I read the job posting! However, I did know that I wanted the job, so I researched SEO online. It turned out that it was what I was already doing with Bleacher Report, but I hadn't known the name for it then.

The real reason I shared that secret with you is because candidates who will dig deep into a new subject and study it to be better at their jobs even if they have no clue what it is are the people you want to hire. You want employees who, when presented with a challenge that might scare others, will say yes to taking it on and figure it out from there.

At the bottom of the posting, Ben included specific instructions on how to apply. He wanted the applicant to include a specific subject line in the email response and to agree to the offered payment. We continue to use specific application instructions in all our job ads to separate the people who pay attention from the losers who don't.

The image of the business that Ben put forth was one of an exciting opportunity alongside hard but interesting work. Not surprisingly, Ben wanted only candidates who were excited about the opportunity and were willing to work hard.

During the interview (to which, if memory serves, I wore a truly awful silver shirt that probably belonged in a disco movie), Ben went over my résumé and asked some general questions about my future plans. It never hurts to hit the standard items, but you should veer off the normal path if you really want to find the right fit. Ben certainly did that when he started talking with me about how I learned things. I told him I was the kind of person who read books and then just tried things. To this day, I have a tendency to run headfirst into a problem and try solutions as quickly as possible while learning more about it along the way. This is particularly true in my approach to learning software. I essentially just keep pressing buttons until I find what I'm looking for, then I trace my way back to where I started. I make errors, and things get messy, but I always end up discovering things that no training manual could have taught me. Let's call it training by breaking things.

At the end of the interview, Ben gave me a copy of Bill Glazer's fantastic book *Outrageous Advertising That Is Outrageously Successful*. I read it in the next 24 hours. Within 72 hours, I was offered a job with Great Legal Marketing and BenGlassLaw.

Now I'm here. A lot has happened in between. But let's skip to right now. I've interviewed countless candidates for positions ranging from receptionist to marketing assistant to attorney. Nearly all my hires have worked out splendidly, and that's because I stick to a set of core principles that build upon what Ben started when he hired me.

Now that you've read through my story, I'm going to give you the "meat and potatoes" information (even though I'm a vegetarian, but the nonmilitant variety, so please enjoy your medium-rare filet mignon with rosemary butter and garlic mashed potatoes).

CHARLEY'S TOP TEN HIRING TIPS

1. Remember that when you are creating your job listing that **you are marketing** to find the ideal marketing assistant. Picture the person in your head—his or her traits, background, attitude, skills, etc. Don't overreach and think you're somehow going to hire Steve Jobs or Jeff Bezos. Without some idea of what you want, you won't be able to create the right kind of bait for your prospect.

2. You should always **hire for attitude** over skill set. You can teach people the basics of search engine

optimization, but you can't teach them to be ambitious and positive. Attitude yields potential.

You should always hire for attitude over skill set.

---

3. I've discovered **two magic questions** I ask every candidate during the interview process. Question number one is, "What are you currently reading, listening to, and watching?" This is the best personality question, because the entertainment and information people consume will give you an idea of their personalities. For example, I'm not going to hire a marketing assistant who says he hasn't read a book outside of school since fourth grade. That particular response was actually given to me by a memorable doofus named Chad. I was stunned. It's true; there are idiots among us, and even the best job ads can't thwart the occasional dud making it to the interview stage. (As a side note, I tend to avoid hiring reality-television junkies.)

Question number two is, "What is the worst thing a previous employer would say about you?" Here's the key to this question: ask it and just wait for the response. Don't qualify the question; don't offer the interviewee a way out. Just wait. I've received remarkably honest answers to this question. People have confessed to severe tardiness issues, trouble controlling their emotions, and all kinds of other things that you would never otherwise hear from job candidates. The question is phrased in just the right way so that they can't really "spin" it in their favor. There's no choice but to be honest.

4. Hiring is a **multistep process**. I first do a brief phone interview and decide if I want to talk to the candidate in person. Then I conduct at least two in-person interviews, sometimes with one of them being a team interview. During the team interview, other employees will be present to ask questions. This can help you feel out office chemistry early on. I'm not looking for everyone to be friends, but I don't want to create a potentially caustic situation. At some point in the process of these interviews (either after the first or second interview), I use the next tip.

5. Use a **personality test**. You need some kind of semi-objective eye on your candidates. Getting them to jump through the hoops of going through the test also proves their interest in the position. It will yield information about them that a series of interviews just can't reveal.

   The absolute best testing system that we have used is the Values Profile through Jay Henderson of Real Talent Hiring (RealTalentHiring.com). The system that Jay uses has saved us from bad hires and helped us better manage new employees, since the test provides invaluable information about a candidate's motivators, stressors, and capabilities.

Simply put, no one gets hired by me without going through Jay's test first.

6. You should be **selling the position** to attract the best talent possible. Tell people why your workplace is where they should be Monday through Friday. By the way, if you can't figure out how to sell your workplace, you probably have a culture problem that needs to be fixed. It's worthwhile to engineer the work environment to be attractive to top potential employees.

7. Make the candidate **sell himself to you**. If someone isn't trying to sell you on his qualifications, he's going to completely flop in marketing. This rule just makes plain, obvious sense. You can even say, "I'm going to give you the last three minutes of this interview for you to sell me on why you're the best person for the job."

8. Sometimes, you just need to **trust your gut**. If someone rubs you the wrong way in an interview, you shouldn't hire him even if his résumé is stellar.

9. **Don't hire out of desperation.** If you rush the process and try to skip to the end, you will find yourself in the exact same position before you know it. Or even worse, you will be stuck with a mediocre employee for longer than you should. As Dan Kennedy says, hire slow and fire fast. Speaking of firing …

10. **Don't be afraid to fire**. If it doesn't work out, it doesn't work out. Cut ties; give someone else the opportunity. Marketing jobs are interesting, and there are plenty of people out there who would love to get their first go at it under your tutelage.

Don't hire out of desperation. If you rush the process and try to skip to the end, you will find yourself in the exact same position before you know it.

CHAPTER 23

CREATE YOUR OWN MARKETING PROGRAM

STEP 1: OPEN THE TOP OF YOUR LEAD-FLOW FUNNEL

Renegade lawyers understand that having a huge lead flow of potential clients will allow them to pick and choose with whom they *decide* to work, and that newfound ability will lead to happier lives for them. They also know that offers of "Call now for a free consultation" or "We'll do it cheaper than the rest" are old-fashioned and self-limiting. Renegade lawyers open the top of their funnels wide, typically by offering books or free reports they have authored instead of (or at least in addition to) any "free consultation." The potential client is then drawn through a sophisticated marketing funnel, one that convinces the right clients that the lawyer is the wise man at the top of the mountain. Such clients will come to those lawyers pre-sold on hiring them.

Consumers in need of legal services generally go through a "moving parade of interest." They might, for example, try to solve their problems themselves by conducting some hit-or-miss research on the Internet. Then, they might decide they need an attorney, but find themselves bewildered by the array of choices (all, by the way, shouting essentially the same message) and in need of a guide to finding the right lawyer. Heck, they might discover you and fire their current lawyers!

Problem is, you don't know what stage they'll be in when they finally come across your marketing. Most lawyers have one message: "Hire me now!" Lawyers who understand direct-response marketing develop marketing pieces, for example, that explain which situations do and don't require a lawyer and help consumers learn how to make intelligent decisions about how to hire the right lawyer for them. Other pieces show consumers how to solve their problems without a lawyer.

Here's how you open the top of your lead flow funnel. Make it easy for a prospect to initiate a conversation with you without having to pick up the phone and make an appointment. You do this by making sure "Pick up the phone and call for your appointment" is not the only "offer" or request for action you make to them with your marketing.

The best way to do this is to create information pieces that answer the likely questions your prospects have no matter where they are on their moving parade of interest. Prepare a free report or book, and then, in addition to marketing your firm, create marketing that's all about the book or free report. Producing and marketing a book instead of or in addition to marketing your firm will change everything because it will help you stand out in the clutter. That's step 2.

STEP 2: WRITE A BOOK

You can't open the top of your funnel without creating books or free reports to offer consumers who aren't ready to "call now." You can create a book in several ways. You can sit down and outline it and then write the whole thing. That's what I did for my original book on car accident cases in Virginia and later for my first lawyer marketing book, *Great Legal Marketing: How Smart Lawyers Think, Behave, and Market to Get More Cases, Make More Money, and Still Get Home in Time for Dinner.* That process, however, can take a long time.

The fastest way (outside of licensing someone else's book to use) is to create an outline of topics, and for each topic, create a bullet list of points that anyone interested in reading the book on your general topic (divorce, personal injury, disability claims, and so on) would want to know about. Then team up with someone who will record an interview with you about each topic. That will be easy. After all, you're the expert and know more about your area of the law than anyone else. (I wrote a nursing home book exactly this way.)

Next, you have the interview transcribed. I like Rev. com, but you can find other transcribers on Elance.com or Odesk.com. Once the transcript comes back, you can edit and rewrite to your heart's content, as the bulk of the work will be done. Better yet, pass it off to a professional editor or ghostwriter for some fine tuning. There are a ton of great editors and ghostwriters around the country and the whole world who can help get your book about 85 percent of the way to the finish line. (The editor of this book, Martin

McHugh, is excellent. You can contact him at agoodeditor@ gmail.com.)

Remember, we're not talking the great American novel here; we're talking about creating an information "premium" you can use to send to potential clients and referral sources that establishes you as an authority on the subject. You don't want a dense, legal tome with 288 fine-print case citations that would put them to sleep. Stop talking like a lawyer. Use infographics to explain big-picture concepts.

The next step is to make your book look good. I highly recommend not doing the final formatting yourself. Again, your time will be better spent by hiring an expert graphic designer for the inside and the outside of the book. Keep in mind that the cover is critical. I use and recommend Kia Arian for this, though you must be a member of Great Legal Marketing to get her to work for you. Kia does all my graphics work. Her work is terrific, and that's because she understands what we want to accomplish. (Read Kia's chapter 30 in this book, "The Use of Graphics and Layout in Law Firm Marketing.")

Once your book is designed and ready to go, have your local copy shop produce 50 copies on regular copy paper, reproduce your front and back covers in color, and then spiral bind the whole thing. Distribute the copies quickly and freely to your friends, and ask them for their feedback. Consider them your behind-the-scenes team of critics, editors, and proofreaders. You'll be amazed at how much useful information you'll receive that will make your book so much more interesting and easy to read. Then you can go ahead and have your publisher fire up the presses to create professionally bound, great-looking books.

Again, you're not writing an encyclopedia of law, and you're not trying to impress fellow lawyers—so write to your ideal clients. Focus on writing something that will interest and inform, nonlawyers and answer some of the basic questions you know they have. Go one step further by answering other questions they might not even know they should have. You'll thus make them take the next step—to the next level in your sales process. For my firm, that means reinforcing the notion that they made a good choice in contacting us in the first place. My books tend to repel those potential clients who wouldn't be good for my firm, but for those who fit our perfect client profile, the book acts like superglue. (You can download copies of my copyright-protected books at BenGlassLaw.com.)

When it comes to conjuring a title for your book, take a gander at what titles have already been taken. Study the "best seller" lists for inspiration. My original book for personal injury cases was *Five Deadly Sins That Can Wreck Your Virginia Accident Claim* with a subtitle that included the phrase *The Ultimate Guide.* Don't copy that! Come up with some new titles (engage some pro editors in that creative process), and remember that the subtitle is just as important. It's also a good idea to check out to see what URLs are available that may match any titles you come up with. For example, I own TheAccidentBook.com.

What do you do with the book once you finish it? Everything. Once you have copies of it in hand (or available in electronic format), you'll change the way you market your practice. No longer will you have to run print ads, create TV commercials, or develop webpages that talk about how great you are (and you know how much the bar loves it when you do that); you'll be able to talk about your book and how useful and informative it is.

What do you do with the book once you finish it? Everything.

Generally, ethics rules limit comparative statements that you make about yourself or your services. This, however, is a book. While the book itself is likely subject to your state's lawyer advertising rules, your ad about the book is likely not. (Read that sentence again and think it through. It's a major point to understand.)

Study great print ads and Internet ads for books. How does John Grisham's publisher market his latest? Grab some ideas from that industry and use them. *Read Me: A Century of Classic American Book Advertisements* by Dwight Garner and *1001 Ways to Market Your Books* by John Kremer are excellent sources of inspiration for book marketing. Normal lawyers will never read either of those two books.

You'll find that your own book is the greatest business card ever invented. Right off the bat, your book will give you a good excuse to issue a press release. A book shouts that you're an authority—*the* authority, even though you can't say that yourself. Your book can be the centerpiece of your marketing efforts and be included prominently in your "shock and awe" package, the info you send out to those who call you for the first time. You'll also want to mention your book in every subsequent press release you issue in which you comment not only on your own cases but also on other relevant news in your area.

Does your message **stand out**?

Whenever anyone calls your office to inquire about your services, your staff can ask, "Did you know Mr. Glass has written the book on car accident cases in Virginia? We'd be very happy to send you one." Your book becomes the perfect reason to request full contact information from your prospective clients and allows you to start marketing to them via multistep and multimedia follow-ups.

You can also send your book to potential sources for referrals. When we review a new personal injury case, we routinely mail a copy of our personal injury books to treating physicians whose names appear in the records and include this letter:

Dear Doctor,

As you probably know, I'm representing Mrs. Smith in her car-accident claim. While going through her records, I saw you were one of her treating physicians. I'm enclosing a copy of my book, *The Five Deadly Sins That Can Wreck Your Accident Case*. This book may be helpful to your staff and other patients. If you would like more copies, just use the enclosed fax-back form.

Ben**Glass**Law.com

☑ Yes, Ben, our office would like ___ copies of

The Ultimate Guide to Accident Cases in Virginia: The Five Deadly Sins That Can Wreck Your Accident Claim.

Please send them to my address below:

Name |
Firm Name |
Firm Website |
Address |
City | State | Zip |

I have a question. Please contact me by calling:

Tel |

BENGLASSLAW.com

My MasterMind member Charlie Hofheimer has been using his books for years to market his divorce practice to family therapists in the Virginia Beach, Virginia, area. All the therapist has to say is, "Here's a book that may be helpful to you"; the therapist doesn't have to actually recommend Charlie's services. (In chapter 27, "5 Reasons Why Clients *Don't* Refer," you'll see how important it is to make it easy to refer people to you. A book is the easiest way for someone to make a referral.)

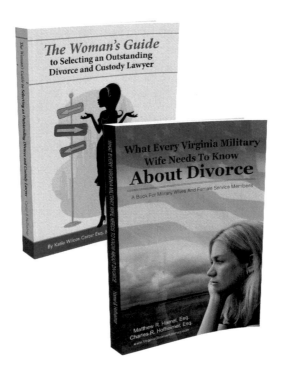

Two Books from MasterMind members
Charlie and Kristen Hofheimer

After you've created your book, you should develop collateral media such as bookmarks, flyers, and ads that advertise your book or books and one-page landing pages for your website that focus solely on each book you produce. You should buy as many relevant URLs as you can to use in your marketing so that responses to your print, radio, and TV advertising can be carefully and specifically tracked.

Here is the landing page for TheDisabilityBook.com.
Feel free to download the ebook!

Your overall goal is to reduce the initial reluctance potential clients might have to raising their hands to contact you. Your book gives them the perfect excuse to get started in a relationship with you.

Of course, the hard part about this is getting the book done. We have books that we license to our membership, but the best book will be the one you create yourself. However, waiting until you get around to it is deadly. In fact, that's a game losers play. Do something!

Finally, the centerpiece of your waiting room can be a stand, or a rack, or a table filled with your books and your books only!

STEP 3: INCREASE THE VALUE OF EVERY LEAD YOU GET

Almost any law firm's ROI on its marketing spend could be improved without shelling out another dime simply by maximizing the potential of the leads it's currently getting. You should have tracking in place that can help you determine the cost of that lead. If you don't have follow-up that can track down the unconverted leads, you're burning money.

Nowadays, you simply need software to run your marketing for you. What's your existing follow-up system? Does it allow you to easily capture contact information for every lead? Is it multistep? Multimedia? This can be done with notecards, but today, most firms use database management software to manage their follow-up marketing. Most case-management products won't run the sophisticated, segmented, follow-up marketing you need to conduct to get maximum potential out of each new and existing contact. Does it run automatically? If not, look at a product like Infusionsoft, which has been running the marketing for smart lawyers for many years (GLMLovesInfusionsoft.com).

The problem most firms have is that after getting a call or a web response from a potential client, they have no follow-up system in place, thus leaving it up to the caller to "get back to them." These firms are missing gold right at their feet. Renegade lawyers continue to reach out to prospective clients in interesting and effective ways that include snail mail, email, and the phone.

Note that this follow-up marketing should *not* be about you; it shouldn't be designed to pressure a potential client into signing up with you. Rather, it should be an effective stream of interesting content that ideally enters the conversation the prospects are having with themselves as they contemplate their legal situations. This is a critical point: such follow-up must be crafted with specific prospects in mind. For example, if they began their search for information on how to settle their own personal injury cases, your follow-up information should be mostly tips on settling their own cases. This is what all the nonlawyer marketing gurus will never get because they haven't had thousands of conversations with real legal clients about what really runs through their heads as they seek out a lawyer. Great Legal Marketing, because it is for solo and small-firm lawyers and run by a small-firm attorney, understands this completely. We are, in reality, running a giant laboratory of lawyer marketing.

Don't worry about giving away too much information. If they can settle their own cases, they were likely too small for you, but you'll still have turned a potential client into an evangelist. Evangelists do cool things for you, like bragging about you to their friends, posting positive comments about you on lawyer rating sites, and "defending" you when inevitable negative comments get posted.

Besides, many of them will discover they just can't settle their cases without a lawyer. Whom do you think they'll call to handle their cases, the lawyer who sent them one follow-up or the lawyer who sent them a steady stream of helpful tips and videos about settling by themselves?

Most lawyers give up way too early on their follow-ups. "I called them back and sent them a package, but they didn't get back to me." That's giving up way too early.

Look outside of the legal industry. Many successful businesses have a "sales force" that tracks down every lead until it's 150 percent clear the lead has no immediate value. Of course, most lawyers don't think in terms of a sales force and leads, but they make a mistake by shying away from basic business principles just because they don't like the labels. Let's just call it a "follow-up campaign."

At BenGlassLaw, some of our best clients (clear liability, substantial injury, and good insurance all around) can take up to 12 months to hire us after they've entered our marketing funnel. There are many reasons why consumers who may end up needing a lawyer to solve their problem are not ready to hire a lawyer today. An interesting and informative follow-up campaign will make sure that you are top of mind when they decide to take the next step. Be persistent. Be helpful.

Here's one simple tactic you could add to your marketing arsenal: a telephone follow-up system for all new leads. This could start with a call about five days after the first contact with your law firm, asking the prospects if they had any questions about the information package they received. You will learn something from that call.

If that call doesn't result in an appointment, the results should be a package of materials mailed to the prospective client's home, this time responding to what it is you learned on the phone.

Five days after that package is mailed, another call is made that goes something like this: "Hello, Mrs. Smith. I'm Suzy from Ben Glass's office, and Ben just asked me to give you a call to make sure all your questions have been answered." Record the call and the answer in your marketing database. Don't leave this to an email auto-responder. It's what average lawyers do and it's just not good enough.

To make this technique successful, you need someone who's great on the phone, good phone scripts, and a database into which all this contact information can go.

STEP 4: PUBLISH A NEWSLETTER

Next, develop a newsletter. (I go into how to create a quality newsletter in chapter 28, but here I'll mention how a newsletter fits into your marketing campaign.) Don't just slap your name on some canned articles; that's a horrible waste of money. Instead, write about what's going on in your firm, your community, and your life. People will do business with people they're fascinated with, so don't pass up opportunities to be fascinating in your newsletter.

Whether or not potential clients become real clients, renegade lawyers continue to market to them and all their other leads via interesting monthly newsletters. A good rule of thumb is that newsletters should contain no more than 40 percent legal information, and they shouldn't look (and definitely not read) like legal briefs. Scope out magazines and newspapers from a newsstand rack that sell well. What makes people pick them up and buy them?

A well-written, monthly, printed newsletter mailed to all your contacts will help convert prospects into clients, and it will also drive referrals. Lawyers who publish great newsletters often include articles about or even by other (noncompeting) lawyers in their locales.

By the way, many lawyers shortcut this critical newsletter strategy by relying solely on electronic newsletters. If that's all you're going to do, you're wasting your time. Electronic newsletters don't get opened, read, and passed around as much as do paper newsletters delivered by regular mail, so use an e-newsletter only as a supplement to a mailed newsletter.

I'd go so far as to recommend you don't spend another penny on marketing until you have your newsletter up and running and a marketing database in place, which I'll address next. (If you'd like to see some samples of the BenGlassLaw monthly newsletter, fax a request on law firm stationry to 877-576-6752.)

STEP 5: CREATE ONLINE AND OFFLINE MARKETING THAT DRIVES REQUESTS FOR YOUR BOOKS

In my market today, nobody (besides lawyers who have come through my system) is offering books and information instead of or in addition to legal services in their *initial* marketing efforts. All of *their* ads are about the lawyer. Offering books and information has served us very well, and the overwhelming response of clients (and even potential clients who don't make it through our screen) has been very positive.

When you change the game by marketing *information* rather than *services*, you gain a huge advantage for yourself on several fronts. First, as I mentioned earlier, you can call your book, website, report, newsletter, and so on "the greatest" and not get yourself into ethical problems because you're not calling yourself or your services "the greatest."

Second, you'll develop higher-quality clients when you lead them through your hoops. I know that idea runs against the deep thinking of most lawyers, those who truly believe that if they don't get on the phone right away, the client will go elsewhere. I believed that, but nothing says you can't do both (send information and schedule them for an appointment) at the same time. The experience of many of our members is that the worst leads, at least in the personal injury field, are those folks who are sitting at home, watching TV, and calling as soon as a lawyer ad runs.

Third, the information you send out, particularly your book, can do the heavy lifting when it comes to managing client expectations. Remember, this is usually their first experience with the law; they know only what friends and family have told them about what to expect once they step into the legal arena. You give them great, full, information in the meeting and you back it up with your book. No longer can they come back to you and say, "Well, you didn't tell me about that part of the law." It was all in your book!

The hardest part of lawyer marketing is standing out from the crowd. How many different ways can you say, "I can help you with your divorce" or "Arrested? We're aggressive"? When you think about the messages to get your book, informational book CD or DVD into people's hands, it's so much easier. For example, you can craft 20 specific messages, each one based on information in your book, and make them blog posts, postcards, and so on. Each one can enter the conversation going on in a potential client's head.

I still hear too many lawyers object that they want to market their services rather than to market information. They cite a variety of reasons, most of which revolve around some notion of "That's too slow of a process."

The point they're missing is that all their leads, whether they turn into cases today or not, have a lifetime value. Most other businesses talk about the lifetime value of their customers or clients, so why not lawyers? All lawyers want new clients, but every single person who comes down your marketing funnel has a lifetime value. If your lead-generation marketing is any good, you may find your ratio of leads to clients is over ninety to one; it's certainly like that in my practice. But my websites (see chapter 32, "Multiple Websites or One?" on this) generate a torrent of lead flow, and that allows me to select which clients I'll take. And I end up with a lot of those "ones."

So what's the value of the 90 percent? Let me count the ways. They have value in that while they might not be perfect for you, they may be perfect for another attorney, and that could result in a referral fee. MasterMind members Bob Battle (BobBattleLaw.com) Tim Miley (MileyLegal. com) (with Susan Miley running the logistics) and Stuart Carpey (CarpeyLaw.com) have mastered the art of carefully and professionally moving cases *out* of their offices to other qualified attorneys. They each have also developed a fantastic follow-up system that ensures that they get paid (when appropriate), that the client is happy (very important), and that the lawyer who got the case knows exactly where it came from and ends up happy. This is "business within a business" stuff.

The second and third values of leads that don't turn into clients is that if you handle them appropriately and professionally, they'll become evangelists for your firm and even referral sources. The evangelists might not ever directly refer, but they could have their own media in which they can promote you. Other small-business owners, reporters, judges, and court personnel come immediately to my mind when it comes to referral sources. Long-term referral sources (mavens) are those who love you, will accurately tell your story, and will know exactly who you're looking for and actively refer people to you.

On the other hand, if you're marketing for cases only, you'll get only those raising their hands who believe they have cases and are ready to start searching for an attorney. Keep in mind they're just a small part of the universe, but that's exactly what normal lawyers go hunting for with their advertising.

When you make your information available through books, reports, newsletters, videos, and the like, you open up the spigot much wider, and that reduces your overall cost per lead. Properly handled, the 90 percent who don't become clients may become worth much more over the long run than the client you signed up for his one and only case in his lifetime.

STEP 6: CREATE A "SHOCK AND AWE" MAILING

Focus on creating a multistep, multimedia follow-up system that begins with a "shock and awe" package so you don't run the risk of giving up on your leads too early.

A "shock and awe" package is simply an initial mailing sent to people who have contacted you and said, "I want more information." The package is designed to impress and may include:

1. Your book (e.g., *How to Get Your Workers' Compensation Benefits in Alabama*)
2. A CD (generally an interview of you about workers' comp claims in Alabama)
3. A book or report about *How to Find the Right Workers' Compensation Lawyer for Your Case*
4. A set of testimonials
5. An informational DVD
6. A cover letter emphasizing that the prospects were really smart to ask for this information and reminding them that you and your staff are there to answer any questions they have.

Here's the key. The information in the package is more information about their problem than it is bragging about you. Sure, you want self-promotional material to be included, but this package will show up like no one else's and, by demonstration, will show you're an expert in your field.

Cost too much? You need to know the value of each case and the lifetime value of every contact in your database. You don't have to start big, but you should do something other than just sending a "Thank you for contacting us" letter.

Here's what you do after that mailing, remembering the principle that you don't want to give up on leads too early.

1. Send three to five email auto responders with additional reports spaced out over the next four weeks. The focus of the emails is always on them; don't yell, "Hire us!" because that comes off as desperate.

2. Send out at least three snail mailings that include some of the same information and some different information. For example, many personal injury and workers' compensation attorneys have additional reports about dealing with health insurance companies, subrogation, and how to deal with health care providers during the claim.

Most Great Legal Marketing Diamond Elite Coaching and MasterMind members who do this well have exhaustive follow-up campaigns. Sure, some cases are characterized by shorter deadlines (traffic accidents, DUIs, and often bankruptcies), but even those lawyers have sophisticated campaigns that separate them from everyone else in their markets.

A word of warning: check from time to time to make sure what you think is happening with your marketing steps is indeed happening. As your marketing gets more sophisticated, your campaign sequences should be double checked against the feedback you and your staff are hearing about your materials.

Yup, it's complex to design and then put into effect a good marketing and follow-up program. But it's well worth it.

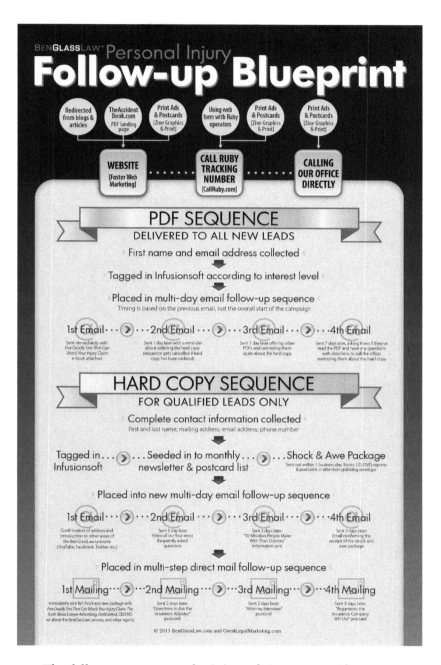

The follow-up sequence for injury claims at BenGlassLaw.

CHAPTER 24

LAUNCHING YOUR MARKETING CAMPAIGN

So I've given you the formula, but don't drop the ball on the hard parts because that separates the winners from the lazy. At our firm, we start all our marketing campaigns with three questions. Diagram this on paper before ever spending one minute creating an ad, TV/radio script, or webpage. These questions are critical to marketing success:

1. What do we want the person who notices this piece of marketing we are about to produce to actually do? Obvious answer: call us for an appointment. Some will, but I hope that I have made the point that there are many who aren't ready to call you for an appointment today, even though they have a problem you could help solve.

2. What do we need to build via Internet landing pages and/or telephone answering scripts to get them to do that? Lawyers will spend thousands of dollars on an ad campaign yet give no thought to the marketing

collateral that must be built to support the ad spend. There is no class for this in law school or at your local bar association meetings.

3. How will we follow up with those who reach out and respond, whether or not they hire us today, and how much of this process can we automate through software such as Infusionsoft?

Unless you get this part right, you're leaving money on the table every time you run an ad. If your ad gets a bunch of folks to actually call your office or fill out a web form but you have no script and no planned, automatically executed follow-up for those who don't make an appointment right when they call, then you're not maximizing your return on investment for the ad. This is okay if done by deliberate choice (and you have money to burn), but most solo and small-firm lawyers like to get the biggest bang for the buck they can.

Most lawyers get all excited about the "creative"—a cool, new website, TV ad, banner ad, or pay-per-click, but they have nothing behind their curtains! This is what makes our style of marketing stand out for those who are willing to do the unsexy, behind-the-scenes work. Rejoice if you are a member of that band of renegades who have true initiative.

CREATE A PLAN FOR ATTRACTING REFERRALS

You cannot create evangelists for your firm by random behavior. You do so by identifying your top referral sources (and potential referral sources) and asking yourself, *What can I do for them today?* Here's what you can do:

1. Use your database to collect and organize information on your clients and prospects.

2. Ensure that your staff reaches out to clients at least once a month for reasons *other* than issues having to do with their cases. And send your potential referral sources something as often as you send things to the rest of your herd. This argues for perhaps a special newsletter just for those who refer. If they're business owners, you could send them a marketing tip of the week or month. MasterMind member Jim Dodson (JimDodsonLaw.com), a personal injury attorney in Clearwater, Florida, holds marketing and practice-building seminars for probate and estate planning attorneys in his area. Charlie Hofheimer has done marketing webinars for the therapists who refer women to his law firm for divorce and custody issues. At BenGlassLaw, we open our video studio to local small businesses to use, and we do video interviews featuring their businesses. We don't charge for this and we ask for nothing in return.

3. Make sure your referral sources know about and even have copies of your series of educational books they can give to friends who may be in need of your

services. You might even create a sticker for the book: "Free Gift from [name of their business]."

4,   When someone does refer a potential client to you, make a big deal about it. Send personal, hand-written thank-you notes and make the referral sources (and their businesses) celebrities in your newsletter. This is easy: find out the anniversaries of their businesses, find out what they do on a volunteer basis for your community, and so on. You can profile them as fellow small business owners in the area who are making a difference.

I go into more detail on this topic of referrals in chapter 27, "Five Reasons Why Clients *Don't* Refer," an important topic in itself.

CHAPTER 25

SCRIPT YOUR STAFF'S TELEPHONE RESPONSES TO POTENTIAL CLIENTS[2*]

Renegade lawyers allow only highly trained personnel who use carefully crafted sales psychology scripts to answer their phones. Want to cause yourself indigestion? Hire a company to make and record a series of ghost calls to your firm. If you're like many who have tried this, you'll be horrified to hear what actually goes on in your office just after the phone rings. In our office, every inbound call is recorded and, yes, we review a sampling of those calls every week. Sometimes, we play them during team meetings and ask, "How could we have made this better?"

It's amazing how much time, energy, and money firms put into getting their phones to ring but never consider the *science* of answering the phone. Usually, busy receptionists or paralegals are interrupted from their work to take on what is the most important task of the day: being the first from your firm to speak with new callers!

---

2   * and Then Train, Test, Train, and Test Again!

Prospects calling your firm should end their calls feeling they've just spoken with someone at the *right* place, not that they interrupted someone's "more important" work.

GETTING THE PHONES ANSWERED RIGHT

Here are the problems that plague the phones at most solo and small law firms:

YOUR STAFF ANSWERS THE PHONE AS IF THEY DON'T WANT TO BE AT WORK.

Rachel the Receptionist picks up the phone. She's chewing gum and browsing Facebook. In the most droll yet tangibly annoyed voice, she summons up an "Adams and Associates. How may I help you?" The client on the other end can practically hear Rachel wishing that this call were already over. If you have ever called another law firm (or any other professional office, such as your doctor or dentist) and thought, *Wow, this person sounds bored* or *She sounds like she doesn't care,* how did that make you feel?

That is what's going through the minds of people who call most law firms. Clients today are getting hold of your "Rachel the Receptionist," and despite your ads talking about how much you care or about the high standards you have, Rachel answers the phone as if her busy day was just interrupted.

People pay attention to little verbal clues in the voices they hear; they focus on the tone just as much as they do the words. You don't have the support of a pretty face, lengthy information packets, or fancy graphics to help you out on the phone. If your receptionist is frowning when she answers the phone, the person on the other end will sense that. This problem is solved by carefully scripting what you staff says on all calls and by building in reminders sitting right there next to the phone about how they should sound.

Calls have become easier for my team members because they have been trained how to handle different situations and to turn every call into a sales opportunity, even if the caller doesn't have a case we want. Now, they don't dread the phone ringing. They actually look forward to it, because they have an opportunity to impress both the client and me (they happen to know that we record our calls and review them—and they don't want to disappoint).

YOUR STAFF GETS THE DETAILS RIGHT BUT FORGETS THERE IS A HUMAN BEING WITH A BIG PROBLEM ON THE OTHER END OF THE LINE.

Sometimes, the folks answering the phones rush to get the details and forget about the human on the other end. Prospective clients don't call your office because they've had a great day. For many, their lives suck. In our office, we have many clients with permanent, devastating injuries or who live in chronic pain from multiple sclerosis or fibromyalgia.

Don't assume that empathy is being used with all your potential clients. Surely, your team knows to just treat the person on the other end of the line as you would want to be treated. No, you don't need to baby them or cry with them, but you can't be cold and calculating. So when we listened to a recorded call in a meeting and heard a staff member nonchalantly "mmm-hmm"-ing while someone told them a tough, emotional story regarding a long-term disability claim and problems with the insurance company, my blood pressure started rising.

It's called "compassion fatigue." In many practice areas, your team hears stories of woe all day long and can become burned out. You need to monitor the calls and continually train in order to deliver compassionate empathy all the time.

In our office, collecting information is very important, so we had to engineer scripts that were both compassionate but efficient. You need to decide what this should look like in your office, write it down, and train to it.

YOUR STAFF FORGETS TO SELL YOUR FIRM.

In the rush to get the bare minimum taken care of, your receptionist doesn't actually sell the firm. If the first person a potential client talks to doesn't seem to believe in your abilities enough to brag about you to a potential client, why would anyone hire you? This is where Rachel the Receptionist is at her worst. She views your law firm the same way she views every other law firm (sure, she likes that you're signing her paycheck, but that's what she expects regardless of how well she does her job). Your staff should be telling people *why* they have called the right law firm and letting them know they've made a smart choice.

But Rachel doesn't know how to do this. That's your fault. Rachel thinks selling you means listing off the number of years you've been in practice or mentioning your no-fee guarantee. (Again, that's what she said everywhere else, so she's bringing mediocrity with her to her job with you.)

What you want Rachel to say is, "Mike, I think you've made a smart choice in calling us today. Mr. Adams has years of experience handling exactly this type of case, and I'm confident he can help you with your issue. I've gotten to talk with people like you who have been our clients in the past, and they've all had really great things to say about how Mr. Adams handles his first consultation." You must instill a fundamental change in attitude—the move from just answering the phone to *selling the firm*. That's the culture you want. You want a sales team, not just a receptionist.

If the first person a potential client talks to doesn't seem to believe in your abilities enough to brag about you to a potential client, why would anyone hire you?

YOUR STAFF ISN'T TRAINED ON CLOSING THE SALE.

After getting the details, Rachel the Receptionist might ask, "Would you like to set an appointment with us?" The moment that the potential client says "No" or just "Not right now," she gives up. (And who can blame the person for saying no? At that point, he's probably had the same experience with you that he's had with everyone else—you don't seem special.) That kind of attitude isn't what gets paying clients in the door.

Your receptionist needs to get the next step set up while she has the person on the phone. Whether that's sending that person a free report, scheduling a follow-up call, or finding an appointment time for him, she shouldn't let the immediate opportunity pass by. The best part is that if they become good at using the scripted "selling the firm" lines you give them, closing clients while they're on the phone will become incredibly easy.

There's a funny little trick at work, as well. When the script becomes memorized after repeated use, it stops being a script for your receptionist and becomes just what she says automatically (and she will take ownership of it, thinking it is hers).

Your closing needs to be well rehearsed. And it needs to be prepared for someone saying no at first. There needs to be a level of persistence without a sense of desperation. You can't have leads who went through the effort of finding and calling you get off the phone without some type of follow-up being arranged. Otherwise, you're letting go of your ability to actually get clients. There's also a bit of "secret sauce" that's routinely ignored.

YOUR STAFF ISN'T DELIVERING THE SECRET SAUCE, THE "WOW" FACTOR.

Just adjusting the first four issues a little can set you apart a lot, but aiming for "wow" is what elevates you to dominating your market. Take a look at Zappos, a business that focuses on customer service. Zappos has raving fans because every interaction people have with the company is incredible. They hang up the phone, even after a significant complaint, feeling validated and appreciated.

Zappos' director of customer loyalty has often discussed their service culture. Even when given an opportunity to move their call center services to a foreign country, they knew the value of their phone service was too high to risk a loss in quality in how the customers were treated. So they moved the company headquarters to Las Vegas so they could build on that culture instead.

Additionally, all new hires go through four full weeks of training, with an additional three weeks for contact center employees. They use this time to put a high focus on providing an exceptional experience to the customer. When you call Zappos, you encounter some of the friendliest receptionists you'll ever hear. And it happens because they're well trained and indoctrinated with the company's message of customer service (Zappos fondly says that it's a service company that happens to sell shoes, clothes, etc.). They had a record service call of eight hours and forty-seven minutes—and Zappos actually brags about it, because the company knows it has a customer for life who will rave about his or her experience. In the long run, that one raving fan will be worth thousands of dollars more to them.

FIX THE PHONES!

Arrange for ghost calls to be made to your firm. Read the results and weep. Then shake that off and actually study them with an expert on sales psychology. This will lead you to crafting scripts that will allow whomever is answering your phone to capture both legal (e.g., what you need to know to evaluate a case) and sales information. Mandate that the scripts be followed.

This strategy requires your follow-up as well; arrange to have ghost calls made to your firm regularly, and go back to the basics with any of your telephone answerers who have fallen off your script.

In addition to ghost calls, you should be recording every call made to your office. The mere fact that your staff knows you're recording the calls will help them stick to the script you prepare for them.

NOTE: We recommend Chris Mullins and her company, Intake Academy, LLC, for ghost calls and training for your intake staff. Chris will do a free ghost call and analysis if you call her at 603-924-1640 and tell her you saw this mention.

CHAPTER 26

CUSTOMER EXPERIENCE: CRITICAL FOR CREATING EVANGELISTS

Renegade lawyers study how to improve their clients' experience with them and their firms. Doing a good job is part of that, but that's exactly what your clients were looking for, so consider that ground zero. How do you inspire them to go beyond that and spread positive words about your firm? You do so by looking at every step they've been through in your office through their eyes and by asking yourself, *What can I do to make the process even better, less intimidating, friendlier? How can I make my clients and prospects feel better about the processes we run them through?* Answering those questions will allow you to identify and then eliminate trust-busting steps in your office systems.

Every client who works with your firm will be comparing the level of customer service you offer with what they get at Amazon, Zappos, and FedEx. You should be making note of the experiences you have with other businesses and asking yourself if you could do that better in your law practice. If you want people to feel good enough about you to talk you up and refer friends to you, make sure they have memorable experiences. This doesn't come naturally; just because you have really nice people working for you and they've been working in your office (or other law offices) for years doesn't mean they truly understand what it means to deliver a *great* experience. Most don't.

WHAT YOU CAN LEARN FROM TRAVELERS INSURANCE COMPANY

I recently had to deal with Travelers Insurance Company on my homeowner's insurance policy. A brand-new Whirlpool refrigerator was secretly leaking and had damaged much of our kitchen floor. (Yes, we'd dutifully visited all the refrigerator-rating sites and bought a highly rated model. So much for the reliability of review sites.)

First, we went to Whirlpool and met a level of customer service that was marginally above competent; it left us with a feeling we were being sucked into a process that would take months to resolve. ("Find your own estimator and repair people, send us three estimates and proof you actually fixed the floor, fill out fifteen forms signed in blood in duplicate because we'll lose some, and call us if you can still find our number when that's all done.")

I told Sandi, "Screw it. I'm gonna call our homeowner's insurance company and see what happens." So I called Travelers.

Of course, I deal with insurance adjusters all day long, so I wasn't looking forward to this experience. But I paid attention to every step. Boy, was I impressed!

This was not a huge claim (about $6,000), but every step of the way, I dealt with Travelers employees who were highly trained in the *art* of customer service. The first person I talked to was knowledgeable and sounded pleased to be answering the phone. No longer than 10 (no typo there) minutes after I got off the phone, I had an email with details of the claim, my claim number, and information about the adjuster who would be contacting me. The adjuster contacted me about 30 (still no typo) minutes later.

The next day, she was at my doorstep. She not only accurately determined the amount of hidden damage to the floor, but she had a computer and a printer in her car that printed out the entire claim, had drawings of my kitchen, and was able to print a check on the spot.

During the visit, she handed me a very nice folder that had the "most frequently asked questions" listed inside. Shortly after the visit, I had a survey to fill out. I actually did more than fill out the survey. I was so impressed that I wrote a personal note to the adjuster and her team.

Since this was damage from a new refrigerator, I dealt with the subrogation department at Travelers, and they, too, were not only very knowledgeable, but they also explained everything I needed to do, step by step, and followed up with very clear emails.

So there I was raving about an insurance company in my newsletter! Why was that? Because the professionalism and "energy" I felt each one of these people gave to my claim made me say, "Wow."

Does your team make people say, "Wow"? How many personal notes do you get? Do you even get thank-you emails or phone calls? If all you're doing is your job, no one is going to thank you, and no one will rave about you to friends. They won't even remember you six months after the case is over. (By the way, when you get a handwritten thank-you note, make a big deal of it with your staff. They will then want to make this happen more often.)

If Travelers Insurance can deliver a wow experience on a relatively small property damage claim, think about what we should be doing in our practices. Sure, this isn't advertising and marketing, *per se*. Ignore it at your peril.

Does your team make people say, "Wow"?

I'LL TALK ABOUT THIS DOCTOR (BUT NOT TOO MUCH)

Recently, my 14-year-old, Matt, broke his collarbone playing soccer. It was more a frustrating injury than a debilitating one, but he was off the soccer field for a little while.

His injury took me to the ER and then, a few days later, to a pediatric orthopedist I hadn't dealt with before. While I'm at these places, I mentally take notes, as you should whenever you have a chance to observe any business's or professional's customer service.

First, the emergency department. A greeter met us as the door and told us exactly how we were to sign in. The wait was relatively short in a waiting room that had free coffee, a TV, and some vending machines.

When we were called to register, we were greeted with a smile by an intake person who introduced herself by name. She smiled and engaged with us throughout the interaction. As you know, when you register at an ER, there's a ton of paperwork, including, it seems, two pages of signatures just to check if we're hard of hearing.

When Matt and I went back to the treatment room, we were seen by another intake person, a nurse, a radiology tech and, of course, a doctor. (I thought this was a bit of overkill for a fractured clavicle, but that's just me.)

They all introduced themselves, bantered a bit with Matt, and told us exactly what they were going to do. And at checkout, everything was explained to us, and they gave us a nice package of material (including a "days off from gym class" note without us even asking).

Okay, so what's so special about that? I didn't think all that much of it until I visited the orthopedist's office a few days later. First, the call to make the appointment was a little bizarre. I went through a phone message tree, and after "pressing 2" to make an appointment, I hit 23 minutes of dead silence. No music, no "Your call is important and we are a little backed up here because Northern Virginia just got hit with another snow storm," no nothing.

When a live person picked up, I sensed I had interrupted her day. I've experienced better phone "life" at every car repair shop I've called in the last year. And showing up at the office was nothing special, either. I get it that you might not have the fanciest office (though this is one of the largest orthopedic groups in Northern Virginia), but will anyone here introduce themselves and smile?

It's a pediatric doctor's office. Kids—even 14-year-olds—go there with some degree of trepidation. Outside of the doctor herself, not a single person acted as if he or she was glad to be *employed*, much less to be seeing *patients* that day. The doctor, however, was good. She chatted with Matt and impressed me because she could actually recite a published study on how quickly professional Belgian soccer players returned to action after clavicle fractures! (Okay, maybe that wouldn't have impressed you, but I thought it was pretty good.) Nonetheless, her professionalism and friendliness were simply undercut by the rest of our experience there.

Were someone to ask today, I'd recommend the doctor but warn about the staff. Her practice wasn't the only place we could have gone in a highly competitive environment.

CHAPTER 27

5 REASONS WHY CLIENTS DON'T REFER

In the automobile sales industry, each car sold by an individual salesperson will result—on average—in four additional referrals to that salesperson. In my attorney MasterMind group, members report that as much as 60 percent of their gross income comes from cases referred to them by their past and present clients and prospects. No one in that group reports getting less than a third of his income each year from the "internal" marketing directed at people who already know him.

You know from your own experience that when a potential client is referred to you, that person tends to have a much greater chance of having a case that you're actually interested in and in hiring you; they come presold. When really good referrals are made, they also come understanding how you work and respecting the advice you give them.

How much of your income in the last 18 months came from referral-based marketing? That is, they didn't get to you by seeing an ad or finding you on the Internet. Don't be ashamed or embarrassed if you don't know. Most lawyers don't. However, if you were to go back and track your numbers for the last couple of years, you'd likely find your raw referral numbers don't match that of the typical automobile salesperson and your gross revenues from referrals don't come anywhere near those of my MasterMind group.

Why aren't more of your clients coming from people who know you? If you're a good attorney who does good work, why don't you have a flood of new calls each week from people who have been referred to you?

The truth is that even though we know that a referred client is a better client, most lawyers don't have systems and tools in place to increase referrals. By my observation, there are five main reasons why lawyers don't get more referrals than they're getting:

WHY CLIENTS DON'T REFER REASON 1: THE ENTITLEMENT MENTALITY

I mentioned the entitlement mentality at the beginning of the book. Some lawyers think that because of their expertise and experience, referrals should just happen on their own. "I've gotten great results for my clients, so I simply *deserve* referrals."

That's a huge mistake. That's not the way referrals happen. As I mention elsewhere, just doing a good job for a client isn't memorable, and it certainly won't excite someone to refer.

I've been going to the same dentist for years and years. (Probably 35. Seriously. He was my childhood dentist.) He's always done a great job for me and has a bunch of these "best dentists" plaques in his office, yet I don't go around town bragging about him, nor have I ever referred anyone to him. Why's that? His doing a good job is simply what I expected. There's nothing particularly exciting about him or his office—no "wow" factor.

The fact that you've been practicing for 20 years and have perhaps achieved some of those super-lawyer badges doesn't mean anything to anybody. Nobody gets excited about that except you, your spouse, and the guy who sold you the plaque for $297. Your past clients, current clients, and current prospects don't even know what any of that means. Thinking you deserve referrals won't get you referrals.

WHY CLIENTS DON'T REFER REASON 2: WORKING WITH YOUR OFFICE WASN'T ANYTHING TO BRAG ABOUT

Let me ask you this: when was the last time you had an extraordinary experience at any professional's office? They can be memorable because they can be so infrequent.

I wrote in the last chapter about my son's breaking his collarbone and our experience at the orthopedist's office. At the other end of the spectrum is our veterinarian. The staff there actually acts as if they're happy to see us when we bring our two dogs in. They greet our dogs and usually have some sort of neat treat for them to help relieve anxiety. They always follow up the visit with a phone call, even for routine visits, and they survey us by email for instant feedback on how we thought they did. My wife and I rave to others about our vet and how pleasant our office visits are.

PERFECTING THE EXPERIENCE

My MasterMind members spend a lot of time at our meetings discussing how we can perfect the experience for our clients and visitors. We dig into how the phones are answered and what scripts are used. We ask ourselves what services others are using to record, monitor, and evaluate calls. How does your lobby look? Do you have systems in place to make sure clients never have to call you to ask, "What's going on with my case?" Is your staff reaching out to your clients at least once a month for reasons other than issues regarding their cases? Do you know birthdates and anniversary dates? Do you, the attorney, know anything about their personal lives unrelated to their legal problems?

Little things, I know. But bundled, they make for a great client experience, and great client experiences are followed by more referrals. Your clients and prospects are very poor evaluators of the quality of your legal services. However, they will compare the customer service they get from you with what they get from companies such as Amazon and Zappos.

So are you giving them anything to brag about?

WHY CLIENTS DON'T REFER NUMBER 3: MAKING REFERRALS TO YOUR OFFICE IS RISKY

Have you ever gone to a restaurant based on someone's recommendation and had a bad experience there? What does that make you think about the person who told you the restaurant was good?

Most lawyers underestimate the fear and anxiety that run through clients' heads when they think about referring someone to you. This emotional response is vastly worse if you or your staff has ever done anything to break trust with your clients. Does it take you too long to return phone calls? Are you late for meetings? Do you not get documents out to them when you promised? Are your documents error-prone?

When people you know make referrals to you, they're putting their reputations on the line.

WHY CLIENTS DON'T REFER NUMBER 4: YOU DIDN'T MAKE A BIG DEAL OF IT WHEN THEY DID REFER

I talked about this a bit earlier in the book. Generally speaking, lawyers cannot pay nonlawyers for referrals. Each state's rules vary, but this doesn't mean you can't make a big deal of it when someone refers. Here are some things lawyers with great referral-based practices do to make a big deal of referrals:

- They pick up the telephone and have an actual, enthusiastic conversation with the person who took the time and the risk to make the referral.

- They write personal thank-you notes on personal stationery. Emailing someone a thank you for a big referral should get you fired. Even dictating a letter on your boring legal letterhead is only a step above useless. Take the time to hand write something. Of course, that note will be even better if you've got a great database filled with information about your current and past clients and prospects. Mention something personal to them that shows you actually know who they are.

- They send them a book. We've talked a lot about your being the expert who wrote the book on your practice, but I'm talking about something different here. Many of my MasterMind members keep on hand copies of inexpensive but cool motivational or positive-thinking books. I can't think of a single state whose bar would frown on your sending a positive-thinking book with a note from you to someone who has made a referral to you.

It's even better if you authored such a book. I've written several books about success in general and business success specifically. MasterMind member Brian Beckcom (big-time maritime attorney, Houston. VBAttorneys.com) has written his own success-thinking book that his referral sources love.

- In their newsletters, they mention those who make referrals. I've already talked about the importance of sending a printed newsletter out in the mail every month and we will dig even deeper in the next chapter. Those of us with referral-driven practices reserve space in our newsletters for publicly thanking people for having trust in us. This strategy not only thanks the referrer, but it also continues to teach everyone else who reads your newsletter exactly what type of cases you're looking for. It also shows them they'll be rewarded by recognition when they refer. Finally, it shows them that it's "safe" to make referrals to you.

WHY CLIENTS DON'T REFER NUMBER 5: THEY DON'T KNOW HOW TO REFER

Have you ever found out a friend or former client referred a case to another attorney that would've been perfect for you? When you asked them why they hadn't contacted you, they said, "I didn't know you did those types of cases." It's happened to me before.

Despite everything we do to encourage referrals, one client for whom we were doing a very good job with her long-term disability case referred someone who had been in a bad car accident to someone else in Fairfax. Now, the client was new to our office and hadn't begun to see all the things we do to teach people how to refer. Still, it really pissed me off to see a lot of money walk out the door.

This could be happening to you far too often because your clients, former clients, and prospects don't know the full range of what you can do. Again, you might be assuming that because you practice personal injury or family or criminal law that everyone you meet knows exactly what these terms mean. I used to look at my wife as if she had rocks in her head when she'd tell me people didn't understand what "personal injury" meant. I thought, *Are you kidding? How could people be so stupid?* Then one day, I found out that another potential client had made his way to the law firm down the street for his car-accident case because he knew that lawyer did car accidents but didn't fully understand what my practice areas included.

As my good friend and mentor Dan Kennedy often says, "We should not underestimate the difficulty of the task."

Here's where your book or books come in. I talk elsewhere how they'll be a source of basic information on divorce law, personal injury, disability claims, and so on, you send to prospective clients. They can also be, as I said before, the neatest business cards you'll ever have. In your book on any one topic, you should list way up front the extent of your practice.

I've now written about 15 books, most of them consumer legal books that establish me as an authority in my practice areas of personal injury, medical malpractice, and long-term disability. I've also coauthored a book on nursing home malpractice with a lawyer to whom I refer or act as co-counsel on nursing home malpractice cases. I've written a number of business books and other "success" books. This is worth the work because in almost every conversation I have with potential clients, I can find a nonlegal book I've written to give to them because of something they tell me in the initial interview.

When you have a book, that acquaintance who loves you can't screw up the referral. A book is one of the great referral tools because in that book, you can tell your story accurately. You can, if you are in my world of personal injury, explain exactly what that means. You can talk to the prospective client about statutes of limitations, how to prove damages, and what juries do in your area in ways that even your best friend couldn't adequately explain.

The book is also one of the best referral tools out there because now there's a lower risk in passing your name on to a colleague. Think about it. The person making the referral doesn't have to say, "Ben Glass is a great lawyer and you should give him a call." All that referral source has to say is, "Here's a book that may help you with your situation."

A book is one of the great referral tools because in that book you can tell your story accurately.

CHAPTER 28

YOU NEED AN INTERESTING NEWSLETTER

An interesting mailed newsletter is the other secret weapon of the top members of Great Legal Marketing. I personally reveiw over 50 law firm newsletters each month from members and nonmembers alike. Here are 11 steps taken by lawyers whose newsletters pay for themselves with referrals:

1. **They mail monthly and militantly.** This allows them to be in front of their clients, former clients, prospects, and potential referral sources every month. If you're thinking about why they don't send these via email, stop right now. Think about how many emails you delete every day.

2. **They keep a stack of past newsletters** and mail copies with initial client information packages. We call ours a "shock and awe" package (see the "Shock and Awe" section in chapter 23).

3. **They mail to local media sources** that write about areas of the law their firms practice in.

4. **They write about the interesting cases** they're handling so everyone who receives their newsletters knows the breadth and depth of what they do.

5. **They make a big deal out of referrals** and never forget to thank those who make them by mentioning them in the newsletter.

6. **They celebrate other small business owners and "heroes" in the community.** Here's an easy advanced strategy when you write about, say, a local business in your newsletter: frame a copy of it and go hang it up in the business's office, waiting room, or lobby.

7. **They invite other lawyers in noncompetitive specialties to write guest articles** about their practice areas. An advanced strategy here is to set up a unique tracking phone number so if that lawyer gets a case from the article appearing in your newsletter, you get a referral fee (assuming you meet all the requirements your state has).

8. **They devote less than 40 percent of the newsletter to legal information.** Let's face it—law is boring to most nonlawyers (and to many lawyers). I get a newsletter every month from a firm that must have hired brief writers to write its copy. I use the

firm's newsletter in seminars as an example of what *not* to do.

9.   **They devote 60 percent of the newsletter to articles of interest to their communities.** These articles might be about their children (my nine children's exploits are often featured in my newsletter), your pets, your staff, and even recipes and puzzles—think fun and interesting.

10. **They distribute the newsletter to other businesses** so they can put it in their waiting rooms or lobbies. If your newsletter is interesting, they'll do this.

In short, these newsletters are interesting to read. If you are regularly mailing a newsletter and you aren't getting feedback on it, you need to reassess whether what you're sending is interesting.

And here is their biggest secret to publishing great, powerful, law firm newsletters.

11. **They put their personalities into them.** You have a philosophy about life? About business? About our educational system? About what it takes to be successful? Write about it. Take a position. Sure, not everyone will agree with you, and you may even repel some people. But you'll form a stronger bond with those who agree with you about your philosophy than you would by trying to be everything to everybody. This is an advanced technique. I frequently write

against lawsuits I deem frivolous (remember the foot-long Subway sandwich lawsuit?), most class action lawsuits (Really? You want to send me a coupon because the price of chocolate went up?), and the government's war on wealth creation. You are a lawyer. Don't be afraid to stand out by voicing your opinion on the issues of the day and do not be afraid to be controversial.

CHAPTER 29

MAKE YOUR WEBSITE WORK FOR YOU

Lawyers get all twisted up about Internet marketing. "How do I get to number one?" they ask. "Which firms do the best SEO?"

The Internet is just another medium for broadcasting your marketing message. In reality, it's not much different from TV, radio, print, and direct mail. The problem is that most lawyers (and the firms selling websites) want to go straight to the "tools" without having a firm understanding of marketing. As I mentioned in the disclaimer section at the front of this book, I would be a fool to talk tools here, because in six months, any specific Internet tool might be irrelevant! You need to think in terms of an overall strategy for achieving what you want with your web presence.

Let's get going.

Even though the Internet is rapidly changing, most lawyer websites are still simple, boring, electronic business cards. At best, they're just brag sites about the lawyers. Consumers don't head to the Internet to read about *you* when they have legal problems; they go there to search for *solutions* to their problems.

Renegade lawyers understand the enormous challenges of making their websites work. Search results are only a small part of the total web marketing experience. Smart lawyers know that even after potential clients *find* their websites, they have just seconds to convince them to *stick around*.

Renegade lawyers have moved away from traditional lawyer websites that display logos, firm names, gavels, and information all about the lawyer. Their websites make good use of interesting, provocative headlines, many different calls to action, and offers of abundant consumer information, including videos. They reject the notion that the primary purpose of a lawyer website is to establish the lawyer as a "thought leader." Consumers don't hire thought leaders, they hire lawyers who can get results.

The primary purpose of the website is to generate leads—people who will trade their contact information to you in exchange for information they're looking for. You website needs to provoke a prospect to take action.

MAKE YOUR WEBSITE STAND OUT

Here's some homework: Compare your website to those of your top 10 competitors. If what they say about *their* firms is pretty much what you say about yours, your website won't stand out.

Renegade lawyers study many websites, including websites in different industries, to gather ideas. They create systems inside their offices for coming up with interesting content. Just as they do with their newsletters, they post compelling stories, examples, and information that can't be found on other lawyers' websites.

Pay attention when you visit top nonlegal websites and ask yourself, *What makes these websites so interesting?* You'll be that much closer to making your website stand out and be more interesting to someone who may need your services.

You need a great, inspiring website because people looking for legal services will use the web even after they've seen billboard ads, or have been told by someone about this lawyer or that, or saw an ad on TV. They want to check things out for themselves, and going on the Internet will be one of the steps most people will take.

Here's some homework: Compare your website to those of your top 10 competitors.

You need a great website even if you have a fantastic referral-based practice. Even if people are referred to you, they'll head to the Internet to *confirm* that referral. Several years ago, I was referred to a great private driving instructor for one of my kids. His website sucked. It didn't matter how good the guy was. The fact that he didn't have any good web presence meant he lost our business. (By the way, if you've ever tried it, you'll know that sitting in the backseat while your young ones are learning to drive is more terrifying than any roller-coaster ride. Lucky me. I have only five more to go!)

SEARCH ENGINE OPTIMIZATION

Regarding search engine optimization (SEO), one of the great things about the Internet is that it's very objective. You're either getting visitors or you're not. In the past, there was a lot of emphasis on search terms, and everyone in my practice area wanted to rank highly for "car accident, [my city]." SEO matters, but the issue is far more complex today than it was just a few years ago. Anyone who tells you there's a magic technique to placing well in a search engine and getting leads from your site is a liar. Here's the key: Google wants to deliver a good experience for the end-user searcher. Google doesn't care much about you sitting in your office typing "divorce in New York City" and seeing where you show up.

Were I counseling a solo or small-firm attorney on building a new site, I would say this: focus on coming up with a great direct-response design created specifically to get visitors to stick. For lawyers, this means not using their firm name as a headline, and no silly stock pictures of gavels, flags, or skylines. This is all fluff sold by vultures knowing that you will show it to your spouse and they will approve it because it looks good. Have copy right up front that begins to answer the likely questions anyone who would visit your site would have. A good book to try to find is *108 Proven Split Test Winners* (DotComSecretsLabs.com).

Next, make sure your site allows you to add content on the fly. Until recently, I thought that every lawyer website had that ability until I spoke to several lawyers I met on a marketing listserve who asked for my advice regarding proposals from web developers. For most, all changes had to be run through the webmaster. That's like buying a TV that only gets four channels. You need to be able to add content without getting in the customer service line!

Third, you'll want a site that supports video (and chapter 31 here is devoted to the topic of video). You need to be able to create and upload videos to your site whenever you want. Several of my MasterMind members have video studios in their offices. This allows them to produce video commentary on breaking news. Again, you shouldn't have to be calling your web vendor to upload video!

Finally, your website needs to be backed up by robust database management software. No sense having all those prospects filling out forms and giving you detailed information only to never be able to efficiently retrieve it for future marketing.

OKAY, ONE FINAL WORD ABOUT SEARCH ENGINE OPTIMIZATION

What about SEO? What are the tricks there? Answer: none. The top strategy is to write quality articles and blogs that your best prospects would like to read. In yesterday's world, we'd write for the "spiders" and pack keywords into our articles. Forget about that. The websites that consistently show up at the top of search engine rankings are there because they pump out a lot of quality content written for the consumer.

Today, any lawyer you find positioned above you in the search engine return pages is simply *outworking* you.

CHAPTER 30

THE USE OF GRAPHICS AND LAYOUT IN LAW FIRM MARKETING

Kia Arian, Creative Director and Copywriter, Great Legal Marketing (zinegraphics.com)

(Note from Ben: Kia is the creative genius behind all of the ads shown in the Advertising example chapter beginning on 181.)

I'm a designer, and I love creating beautiful things. The only thing I love more is designing things that actually make money for my clients. Marketing that produces results will rarely win awards and accolades in design competitions. Although this may sound unfortunate for me, thankfully, I have no interest in winning design awards.

My definition of a winning design is one that brings attention to the marketing message, commands the reader's attention, and delivers a response. An effective design will not bring attention to itself. Who wants people "ooohing and ahhhing" at your clever design, only to walk away and never recall your message, your product, or your company?

However, this doesn't mean that your marketing must be devoid of any aesthetics or visual appeal. In fact, countless studies prove how vulnerable our perceptions are to visual stimuli. In other words, the way something looks greatly influences our judgment of it (and in many cases, how we experience it).

When we talk about graphics and layout, we're not just referring to what color something is or how beautiful, balanced, or organized it appears (which are all subjective anyway). We want to know the effect that design elements have on buyer perception, and how to influence those perceptions.

In any marketing, your message is the most important element. A great design can communicate your message in a great way. But, if your message is weak, then a great design is only going to make things worse by communicating a bad message really well.

With that in mind, let's first quickly look at your marketing message and how it should be presented. Then I'll share my favorite tips and strategies for using graphics and layout to give your message some more *POW!*

HEADLINES

Whether you're using a postcard, a print ad, a sales letter, or a website page, you MUST have a strong headline. The headline is the MOST important element in your message. It is the thing that tells the reader whether to stay and read the rest of the message, or to move on.

Learn what makes a great headline and you will increase the readership of your ads by as much as 50% (source Ogilvy, *Confessions of an Advertising Man*). It's not some mystical formula. There are tons of great resources available. One of my favorites is *Great Headlines Instantly 2.1* by Robert Boduch.

IRRESISTIBLE OFFER

Your marketing should always be offering something for your client to buy now or request for free. Your offer should be very specific and, preferably, very targeted to your ideal client. Look at most lawyer ads and prepare to be shocked by how many have NO specific offer. They're merely announcements that the firm exists. Sometimes, they'll tell you their favorite slogan. Slogans don't sell.

CALL TO ACTION

Make sure it is painfully clear what they need to do to respond to you. Do not make it complicated or be timid about it. Be loud, with very clear instructions. Also, responses to your ad should be trackable to the ad. How else are you going to know if the ad is working?

RELEVANT COPY

Volumes exist on how to write good copy for ads. If you're writing your own ads, you will do yourself a disservice if you don't, at minimum, learn what constitutes good sales copy. You can always hire a copywriter. But you should be able to judge whether the copy is good or not. The only other thing I'll say about copy is that long copy (lots of words) has repeatedly and unequivocally been proven to pull more responses and produce more results than graphic-heavy ads with bullet points. If you're still on the fence about that, it's time you stop fighting it and just accept it.

DEADLINE

Ads with a deadline will outperform ads without a deadline. You can do this via an expiration date for the offer, limited supply, or a bonus gift, book or report if they respond by a certain date. Extra-long deadlines reduce response since people will put it off thinking they have time, and then forget. There needs to be a sense of urgency.

GRAPHICS AND LAYOUT

Just like you don't need to be a copywriter to recognize good sales copy, you don't need to be a designer to recognize good design. However, you do need to be aware of principles of design that make for a great overall marketing piece.

THE ENVIRONMENT OF THE AD

If you are making a print ad for an outside publication (like a newspaper or a magazine) consider the entire look and feel of the publication, and how your ad looks placed in the publication. If possible, send your designer the publication or a scan of the publication, and ask them to place the ad in one of the pages. It's generally a good idea to match the graphic climate of the publication. The reader will subconsciously think it's part of the publication and not an ad. This applies for online banner ads, too.

THE USE OF COLOR

The decision to use color is often a budgetary decision. Although the cost of color printing has dropped significantly in the past decade, black and white printing can still be much cheaper in most cases. It's a known fact that color draws more attention, so use it when you can.

But, there are strategic uses for black and white only printing, as well. Remember, the aesthetics of your marketing is not about how beautiful it looks, it is about the response that is elicited. In the lawyer marketing world, "response" means they picked up the phone or filled out a form requesting either an appointment or more information.

THE USE OF IMAGES

An excellent technique to make your material more persuasive is to add compelling images and photos that support your message. Visual imagery is the most direct path to perception. Pictures of people, faces, and the human form are the most attractive to people. This includes pictures of yourself. As a general rule, you should avoid (or keep to a minimum) stock photos of happy models predictably posed in artificial settings. It's boring and so far from reality that most people just tune it out. Images that are reality, or look like reality, are more interesting. Here's a big tip: every image should have a caption. Image captions are one of the most read parts of any ad!

THE USE OF SUBHEADINGS

Include a subheading, two to three lines, below the heading. And continue to add subheadings throughout the copy. Can you imagine reading a legal brief with no subheadings to break up the text? Good subheadings are like road signs along a road. They help guide the reader and prevent him from getting lost or give up on the task of reading your materials. It also affords "glancers" the opportunity to get your message without reading the entire advertisement.

THE USE OF BRANDING

A consistent branded look is generally good, but branding should not overpower or distract from the message. The purpose of ANY advertisement is to give the reader as much compelling and interesting information about your service so they decide that YOU are the perfect attorney for them. No one ever decided to hire an attorney because they admired the firm's logo. Don't waste valuable real estate by making your logo the biggest image on your ad. "But I want them to remember us," you cry out! The best way for them to remember you is for them to have your consumer books, newsletter, and other educational information in front of them on a regular basis. They will remember you as the expert and the guy/gal who wrote the book on it. It's fine to use your logo, but don't make it the focus.

THE USE OF ARROWS, ASTERISKS, AND MARGIN NOTES

Making "hand drawn" arrows and notes in the margins is a surefire technique for drawing attention and directing the reader to specific parts of the ad. Notes like this add a very personal touch, which is attractive and, in many cases, sets your ad apart. They also afford you the opportunity to add text that would otherwise not fit cleanly in the body of the ad.

THE USE OF REVERSE TEXT

Reverse text refers to using light colored text (such as white) on a dark background (such as black). Please do not ever do this for body copy! It's tiresome to read and hard to focus on. Always set body copy in dark color on a light background. If it's not black and white, make sure there is a lot of contrast! For example, don't put gray text on a yellow background. Using reverse text for titles or short headlines is OK and helpful for drawing attention.

THE USE OF "COUPONS"

Remember those mail-order advertisements that filled magazines before the days of the Internet? Well, studies have shown that they are still effective in drawing attention and getting response. People don't necessarily cut out the mail-in coupon to fill out and mail. But the look of it alerts the reader that there is something to be requested, ordered, fulfilled, and shipped directly into their hot little hands. It sparks curiosity and promises fun, wisdom, knowledge– or all of the above. Even using a graphic of a coupon with dotted lines and an offer can be irresistible. Use it when you can.

These are just a few easy techniques that you can use to graphically enhance and improve the readership and effectiveness of your marketing and print advertisements. For more techniques and tons of examples on effective marketing pieces, you should check out my book, *Five Ways Your Design is Sabotaging the Sales of Your Products and Publications* (www.InfoProductDesign.com).

Beyond your print ads, you should remember that everything visual associated with your services sends a powerful clue about your service. The influence of the visual clues is not superficial; they go to the very heart of your service and your relationship with your clients.

Take an inventory of what clues you are sending. Does your marketing say "struggling attorney" who can barely make ends meet and can't afford nice stuff? Or does it say you believe in your success, and you prove it by investing in it and give others confidence to invest in you as well?

Take an inventory of what clues you are sending.

Do you show that you pay attention to details? That you are trustworthy? Reliable? Or do your marketing materials say your service is haphazard and not put together carefully?

Does your presentation to your client say you care about their experience with you, or you just want to take their money?

These are, admittedly, issues that a designer would enjoy pondering over. You're an attorney, not a designer. Depending on how involved you are in the design decisions, this information should help you make more strategic decisions and recognize good layout from great layout.

Kia Arian is the leading expert in graphic design for direct-response advertising, attorney marketing, and information products. She is relied upon by leaders in the information marketing world and by attorneys nationwide who understand the value of education-based, direct-response marketing. She is also a Dan Kennedy Certified Copy Writer.* Her ability to take *ideas and concepts and quickly turn them into reality with zero sacrifice of tried and true direct-response principles makes her a highly sought-after designer in the world of attorney marketing and direct-response advertising. See her work for Dan Kennedy, Ben Glass, Steve Clark, Chauncey Hutter, and other leading information marketers by visiting her website at www.zinegraphics.com.*

*The Dan Kennedy Copywriter for Info-Marketers Certification is awarded to professional copywriters who have successfully completed a course of study of preparation for such copywriting.

CHAPTER 31

THE FIVE RULES THAT SEPARATE LAWYER VIDEOS THAT SELL FROM THOSE THAT DON'T

Colin Lynch, Writer and Chief Video Producer, Great Legal Marketing and BenGlassLaw

Vulture Video Productions, Inc.
"Where all the messages are the same."

As Ben has mentioned, video can be a powerful marketing and trust-building tool for a solo or small-firm lawyer. As Ben's personal video studio manager, I've got some good news, and I've got some bad news, on the topic. First, the bad:

MOST LAWYERS ARE NOT NATURALS IN FRONT OF THE CAMERA

I've shot, edited, and coached lawyers through my fair share of video shoots over the years. When I first started, I was shocked that even a "tough-as-nails" litigator would freeze up when staring into a camera lens. Lawyers need just as much coaching as everyone else in a video shoot despite any public-speaking or trial experience they may have under their belts. Truth is, most lawyers haven't been in front of a video camera very often.

To top it off, most videos that lawyers post on their websites (sometimes even paid, professional work) are awkward, disjointed footage of uncomfortable attorneys. A lawyer stumbles through a script without vision or purpose, and the result is a video that does not convince a potential client to accept an offer for more information or call the office.

There is hope, however! If you're a lawyer who is nervous about video, you're not alone, and there is a formula to conquer it. Here's the reality of the situation:

1. **Shooting and editing a video is easier than ever.**
   Only 10 years ago, shooting high-quality video meant a $2,000 investment in the camera and equipment. Today, smartphones can shoot and edit videos that,

when done properly, are *more* than adequate for a small firm's Internet marketing funnels. This is great news for solo and small-firm attorneys.

2. **There are strategies for getting authentic footage that converts.** Below, I'll be walking you through the five rules for getting footage that will convince potential clients to pick up the phone. If you're the kind of attorney who's initially nervous about shooting a video, you'll be pleasantly surprised how much your footage improves with just one or two hours of practice, and soon your videos will be out there working for you while you sleep.

3. **The benefits are real.** We wish we could show you how many people have scheduled appointments at BenGlassLaw who felt led to call after watching our videos. "I've seen all of your videos, Ben." "I saw your YouTube stuff and you were the guy I wanted to work with." The effect on the bottom line is real. People feel as though they've met you, and they call your office already convinced you're the lawyer they want on their case.

With that in mind, what videos should you shoot?

THE HOMEPAGE VIDEO

This is your chance to inspire visitors to your website to contact you. This is not the place to brag about yourself, because they didn't go online to find out about you; they went online because they had questions and they believed the Internet was a safe way to get answers. Thus, the homepage video should let the visitor know that you know the questions they have and that they've landed on the right place to find answers. This is the most important video you'll shoot, and it's worth scripting, refining, testing, and refining again. Most marketing vultures will try to convince you that you need to be standing in front of law books, talking about yourself and how much you care. As Ben always tells us in our office meetings, that's nonsense.

FAQ VIDEOS

At BenGlassLaw, most of our best clients end up signing with us six, even up to twelve months after they've first reached out to us for information. This is because most people aren't ready to hire legal help right away; they want to "research" their problem first. If you can reach people at that stage with free, educational material, you'll gain their trust and start to develop relationships with them.

FAQ videos are a fantastic way to do this. They can be placed on your website and inserted into email follow-up campaigns. Start by shooting your answers to the questions you're commonly asked in initial client consultations. Then shoot an FAQ video that answers the questions your potential clients don't even know to ask.

THE BIOGRAPHICAL VIDEO

Okay, finally a video about you! Your biographical video focuses entirely on your story. It can go on your "About Us" page and your Avvo or SuperLawyers profiles. Getting people to know your story and see you as a real person is simply one of the largest factors in potential clients' decisions to call your firm. Don't hold back! Let people get to know you. You'll be floored by how many cases you get due to a casual mention of your favorite hobby or sports team in a video.

Now that you know what kinds of videos you should shoot, here are the five rules that will make your videos convert prospects into clients.

RULE 1: BE AUTHENTIC

This is listed first because it is *the* most important factor in whether potential clients will feel reassured and comfortable enough to call about their cases. There's an old saying about George W. Bush: "Folks voted for him because they felt they could have a beer with him." When it comes to video, it's just plain true. The content you're delivering is equal in importance to your tone and appearance.

I had a shoot with a lawyer once who was a turkey hunter and a Baltimore Ravens fan. He actually said, "I bleed purple during football season and camo during hunting season." He let out a genuine laugh, and I knew right away that was the most valuable footage of the shoot. He got nervous about posting it, but once he did, the response from his friends, family, and clients was so overwhelming that he demanded that clip be edited into *more* videos.

Everyone who saw the video mentioned that portion to him with a huge smile because they felt they had something in common with him—that he was a friend they just hadn't met yet. Potential clients started coming to his DUI firm in Baltimore already convinced he was the lawyer they wanted. That's the power of authentic video.

The lesson: only post footage of yourself in which you're comfortable, reassuring, and not nervous. Practice and prepare as much as you need to achieve that tone, because it's priority one in getting footage that works.

Only post footage of yourself in which you're comfortable, reassuring, and not nervous. Practice and prepare as much as you need!

RULE 2: MAKE A SIMPLE OFFER

When lawyers start out with Great Legal Marketing, we tell them to first create an educational offer for web visitors to raise their hands, accept their materials, and opt in to hear more about their legal problems. Once lawyers get a lot of these educational offers in place, they are excited to show *everything* to a new viewer. That's a mistake.

A confused buyer is not a buyer, and it's hard enough to keep people's attention on a website as it is. You want to pick *one* thing you want the viewer to do next. Whether that's requesting your book to be mailed, or downloading your free report, or calling your office, make it big, obvious, and front and center. This can mean showing your offer at the bottom of the screen for the duration of the video, saying it verbally during the video, and cutting to a final screen that gives viewers the call to action again.

To quote a first-century philosopher, "To do two things is to do neither." Pick one call to action for your video, make it big, and stick with it.

RULE 3: REASSURE, GUARANTEE, AND PROMISE

Put yourself in the shoes of potential clients. Most have been thrust into the legal world involuntarily; this may be the first time they've *ever* thought about calling a lawyer. Depending on your practice area, they may be going through one of the most trying episodes of their lives. To make matters worse, many will have the preconception that lawyers are sleazy, dishonest, and unaffordable.

This means you have to spend time reassuring your viewer. Answer their biggest objections before they even ask them. Explain the benefits of your free book. Explain that a phone call isn't a commitment and that you just want to help them get the information they need. This may sound obvious to you, but for the viewer who's worried and nervous about the process, this language is an essential component in selling the call or click you've arranged for them to take next.

RULE 4: SHOW PROOF

This tip is as old as marketing itself, but we'll keep preaching it until it stops making money (and that will be never): testimonials work.

As with all of the advice in this book, everything should be carefully scrutinized and within your state bar's advertising restrictions, but if you're allowed to broadcast particular case results or get people on video telling their stories of their experiences with your firm, that's plain gold!

When we first started asking clients to come in for video testimonials at BenGlassLaw, we were worried people would be nervous and intimidated. The opposite occurred! Many of our clients were *waiting* for a chance to vent (about their insurance company or their accident, etc.), and video testimonials were the perfect vehicle for them to brag about us and share the stories of their cases.

If there's a moment in your case process when your client is happiest with you and eager to share, ask him to come in for a filmed client testimonial. The added bonus? People who don't want to (or who are bedridden, such as with our long-term disability clients) will often give you a written testimonial in its place that can be leveraged just as much as a video can.

Here's a deep, dark secret about testimonial videos: they're not about you! A video that tells a client's story is much more powerful than a video that simply says, "Ben Glass did a good job for me."

RULE 5: BE ENTERTAINING

This is listed last, but don't be fooled. Whereas authenticity is the most important factor in getting a viewer to take action, entertainment is the most important factor in getting a viewer to continue watching.

No matter how valuable the content of your videos, you have only six seconds to capture a viewer's attention (some research suggests even *less* time). Today's potential clients are so inundated with marketing language and surrounded by so many distractions that you have to take a new approach to this and throw away what you think a typical lawyer video should be.

Have fun! If you think of something big and visual and crazy, get it in your video! Tell stories. Give things away. Interview guests. Give lots of value. The power of a good story alone can get viewers to make it to your offer without clicking on the other twenty tabs they have open and vying for their time.

When you achieve a personal tone for your videos that shows you're fun, relaxed, and informative but serious when you need to be, you'll cultivate a responsive herd that reaches out and sends you quality clients today and referrals tomorrow.

At first, video can seem intimidating—too big of a hurdle to get over. While it's true that videos shouldn't be shot until other systems are in place (offers, follow-up campaigns, direct mail, etc.), once you have a working funnel for potential prospects to go through, video is an essential component of closing the "sale" to book an appointment or request materials. At the very least, you should have a homepage video that reassures visitors they're at the right place.

You shouldn't let the apparent size of this task paralyze you. If you're a perfectionist, put that trait aside and just do it. The only way to get better at video is to try the best you can, analyze, tweak, and try your best again next time. In less than a year, your video quality will skyrocket just through seeing yourself on camera and adjusting your approach. It's impossible to build up to the videos you want without bootstrapping it at the beginning and improving your skills.

I've said very little about video quality and equipment, and that's simply because these five principles overshadow production values. Even a video with poor lighting but an enthusiastic, relaxed attorney will outperform a video of an awkward, uncomfortable attorney, even on a professional, $10,000 set.

I encourage you to simply get out there and start. You'll be amazed with your progress in just a few months, and in the end, you'll have videos doing work for you 24/7 to get that phone to ring. All without consuming any of your valuable time with friends, family, and the practice of law.

CHAPTER 32

MULTIPLE WEBSITES OR ONE?

THE INTERNET IS NOT JUST ABOUT SEO

I'm asked the question about multiple websites versus a single point of entry all the time. I asked around for the thoughts of some folks whose opinions I respect. Opinions abound on this, but here's where I land: create multiple websites, especially if you have disparate practice areas, such as personal injury and real estate.

Hear me clearly. I know firsthand about the time, effort, and money that goes into making even a single site rank well for consumer search. I get it. However, that must be weighed against your need to be perceived as an expert. Having one site with multiple, nonrelated practice areas screams, "I'm a generalist!"

But Googling isn't the only way they find you, is it? They might have found you by pay-per-click, banner advertising, or Facebook ads, or they may have found you by your offline marketing. Regardless of how they got to your site, you have a better chance of getting them to pay attention if what they find at that site closely matches the message that had gotten them there in the first place, front and center, and not buried in a bullet-point list of your practice areas.

Many lawyers make the mistake of buying pay-per-click ads that lure visitors in, only to send them to some nonspecific page at their websites. If you're buying pay-per-click ads and you can afford to send them to a website that is only about the same subject as the pay-per-click ad, you'll have a far better chance of moving them along your marketing funnel.

Only you can make the decision about the allocation of resources to your different Internet properties, but of course, it's all for naught if you don't have an effective, multistep, follow-up system in place. So the principle is *don't* mess with multiple websites until you have a foundation that includes good marketing software and solid follow-up systems in place.

CHAPTER 33

GETTING INTERNET REVIEWS

AVVO AND OTHER "LAWYER RATING" SITES

Renegade lawyers realize serious consumers visit rating sites. You and your team should be maximizing every local search profile you have access to and doing what you can to make yourself attractive on Avvo.com, SuperLawyers.com, and BestLawyers.com. You can ignore all the other lawyer directory sites that tell you, "You can be listed here."

Renegade lawyers leverage these highly popular consumer sites and, yes, they pay for advertising on them. You may think it entirely irrational for a consumer to pick a lawyer based on feedback from anonymous sources on the Internet, but renegade lawyers understand consumer behavior.

DEALING WITH BAD REVIEWS

A law firm here in Virginia sued Yelp after someone posted a negative review about the firm. The firm wanted Yelp to remove the negative comment and sought damages from the person who had made the comment and Yelp. The case was ultimately dismissed, but not before generating more unfavorable publicity, which increased the public's awareness about the bad review.

Less-than-stellar reviews are a risk to any solo or small law firm. A high-end strategy is to develop a system in your office that seeks reviews from your happy clients and potential clients on Avvo.com, Google+, and any other review site popular in your area. The part about potential clients is huge. Encourage those you help, even if they don't hire you, to give you a review. Nothing beats a bad review like tons of good reviews.

How you respond to a bad review or even a fraudulent review is important. First, if you screwed up something, *explain* it in your response. One summer, I bought a used car for one of my kids. There are no fewer than 15,324 used car dealers within five miles of my house, and I chose the one that not only had the most reviews, but had also responded to all the negative reviews in detail and with apologies as necessary. For me, that built trust.

I don't think filing a lawsuit against Yelp or any other review site will do anything other than draw out other crazies who are unsatisfied clients and who may be more prone to then pile on to the negative review. Far better for you to go out to your tribe of raving fans, point out the review, and ask them to weigh in for you.

If the review is total BS, I suggest a long-form response modeled after MasterMind member Bob Battle's (BobBattleLaw.com) response to an unhappy DUI client. I'll give you some excerpts here (used with Bob's permission) from what I call a great response to a negative online review in which Bob avoided violating any of the rules of attorney-client relationship.

> So, after this great week, I see that someone who says he was a client over three years ago decides to tell cyberspace how much I suck! I get that I have chosen to be a DUI lawyer and that it is very analogous to being a sports coach in that way too often, the client's opinion of your services is based solely on the result. You win, you are pulling off "miracles"; you lose, you are a "one star" lawyer. Now I know how the coach of the Brooklyn Nets felt when he was named NBA coach of the month for November and got fired in December when the team lost a few games!

> So, sorry to this poster that the prosecution could prove his guilt and there were no "miracles" to be found. I did my best all the while knowing that as a DUI defendant in Virginia, we were competing on a very "uneven playing field." Virginia is the state where you can be convicted under the drunken driving statute without the necessity of the government having to prove that you were either drunk or driving. Virginia is the state where it is legally "irrelevant" that your

car is not even on, operable, or whether you had zero intention of driving. The state where a sitting judge was quoted in the newspaper that fellow judges had approached him and told him they were unwilling to follow their sworn duty to uphold the Constitution if it would lead to the dismissal of a DUI charge. So to a happy reviewer on this website (i.e., I won his case): "Mr. Battle's no-nonsense attitude is remarkable. He gives it straight and does not sugar coat his thoughts or advice."

You have a choice: you can spend a couple of years and a lot of your time and energy litigating against Yelp, or you can enlist your tribe to answer the response for you and take the opportunity to explain, in an appropriate way, why the client got the result he did.

CHAPTER 34

EVERYBODY'S DOING IT: LINKEDIN

I had a discussion recently with a buddy who said I should be spending more time on LinkedIn. I asked him why, and he said, "Because that's where all the lawyers are, and everybody's doing it."

Really? I would have thought that the answer to the why question would have been empirical evidence such as, "I did this and this last year and landed three cases worth $200,000." I could have accepted an answer along the lines of, "I'm running an experiment testing this and that and measuring results, and I can show you how to run the experiment too. I'd be interested in your results." *Anything* but "Everyone else is doing it." A couple of my kiddos complained that all their friends had gotten iPhones for Christmas while they remained iPhone-less. "Really?" I asked. "Let me call a couple of their parents to check." Turns out only one did. Most of the parents of my kids' friends are smart.

Tell me about how you're spending time on LinkedIn *after* you show me your well-thought-out system for generating referrals from lawyers in your area. Show me your program for doing something for those (noncompeting) lawyers first, things like articles about them in your newsletter or a system for having them show up on your videos.

Do you know the names of the folks answering the phones at their offices? Show me you have a way to transfer hot leads to them if you get a call from a potential client who needs their particular services and that you have a follow-up system for making sure the lawyer and that referral had a wow! experience with each other. Show me you touch base with your referral sources every so often for reasons other than "Refer me another case." Heck, show me that you even have a list of lawyers who referred to you and lawyers you made referrals to in the last year and that you know which of your referral sources made you money last year.

LinkedIn is the Yellow Pages gone digital. It's the chatter in the halls at your local CLE course. It's a huge time suck unless and until you've done all the hard work above to create real relationships. Even then, I could show you something better to do with your time.

CHAPTER 35

BONUS CHAPTER: THE PURPLE PILL TO SOLVE ALL YOUR PROBLEMS

One more thing about marketing: most lawyers having read this book will say, "That's way too much work." What they're looking for is the purple pill, the one thing they need to know to market better. Renegade lawyers embrace the complexity; they know that most other lawyers say they're ambitious but aren't willing to do the necessary work.

But if you do want the *one* thing you should do, here it is:

THE ULTIMATE FLEXIBLE MARKETING SECRET TO CREATING YOUR PERFECT PRACTICE

You need to know all the ways (media, including referral sources as media) and reasons (what provoked them to think "lawyer") those who are your avatar clients find their way to you and the questions they try to answer for themselves before being provoked enough to think "lawyer."

Okay, there's one other step: create initial marketing pieces (headline, content, call to action, "offer") and extensive, multistep, multimedia follow-up sequences for each practice area that will convert someone who has discovered you into a client to whom you can deliver an excellent legal result and top-level customer service. You'll convert them into one of your raving fans to whom you market forever (newsletters, new books) and manage with a fantastic marketing database.

Sound complicated? It is. But driving clients to your practice is worth the time and money. It's the lifeblood of your law firm. Renegade lawyers understand that more than anything, and they're willing to put in the hours to make it happen while other lawyers aren't.

CONCLUSION

What I've given you in this book are simple and easy tools that most every successful solo and small law firm I know uses to increase referrals, get better clients, and, yes, make more money while still getting home in time for dinner.

The difficulty is that developing and implementing all these tools, simple or not, can at first blush seem a daunting task, and that will put off a good number of lawyers. But that will definitely work to your advantage if you take it step by step; you'll leave lazy lawyers in the dust.

I've given you a bunch of do's: review the systems you have (or don't have) in place. Figure out what you can do better in your practice. Tackle the chores I've given you one by one (creating a compelling newsletter, writing a book, be on the lookout for great websites, and so on—they're all in this book). Learn to delegate whatever and whenever you can.

I've also given you a bucketful of don'ts: don't let time vampires drain off that precious resource. Don't hold on to clients who just aren't right for you and your practice.

Again, in the book. Focus on taking some steps daily; your efforts (and those of your staff) will add up, and you'll go from "Can I actually accomplish this?" to "I just did it!"

Do you want to craft your own existence? It's all in your attitude. I'm here to say that success using my methods is achievable. I know this personally, and I also know an impressive number of lawyers in Great Legal Marketing who know, this as well.

You want a successful, rewarding legal career that will let you get home in time for dinner and go to your kids' soccer games, guilt free? It's yours for the asking.

ADVERTISING EXAMPLES FROM
BenGlassLaw

Here are some samples of actual ads we have used at BenGlassLaw. Some of these examples may have outdated phone numbers or landing pages by the time you read this book. Please note that all of these examples are copyright protected and some are licensed to members of Great Legal Marketing. Now is a good time to go back and read the disclaimer at the front of this book!

Here's an older ad that still makes me chuckle. When the Virginia State Bar read it, I was told I had to increase the font size of the "Legally, we can't say . . ." line. I did. But that didn't change the response rate at all; the readers knew exactly what we were doing and probably chuckled, as well. Take a look at that "Outrageous guarantee" line way at the bottom, another hook and another point of contact we offer readers.

KNOW SOMEONE WHO NEEDS OUR HELP?

Our best clients come from YOU—the folks who know us and trust us.

If you know someone who needs our help, the best thing you can do is give them one of our books. Circle each of the books that you need.

| **The Truth About Lawyer Advertising** | **GetItSettled:** The Accident Victim's Guide to Settling Your Case *Without Hiring a Lawyer* | **Why Most Medical Malpractice Victims Never Recover a Dime** | **Robbery Without a Gun:** Why Your Employer's Long-Term Disability Policy May Be a Sham | **Five Deadly Sins That Can Wreck Your Injury Claim** |

YOUR INFORMATION HERE *(so we can rush your books to you)*

Name: _____

Tel: _____ Email: _____

Address: _____

_____

Drop this card in the mail (no postage necessary) or fax to 703-783-0686. Or, scan this card (or take a picture with your phone) and email to staff@BenGlassLaw.com You can always call us with the referral at 703-544-7876.

BenGLASSLAW™

3915 Old Lee Highway, Suite 22B
Fairfax, VA 22030 • *www.BenGlassLaw.com*

Here's an example of a freestanding insert we put into our monthly newsletter we mail out. And all lawyers should have a monthly, mailed-out newsletter. Ours goes to our "herd," so to speak, to let them know all the ways they can make referrals to us. They can get books mailed to them by faxing us this form, scanning and emailing it to us, mailing it to us, or just calling in. Any one reader might be a long-term disability client of ours, but this lets him know we also handle malpractice cases and so on if he knows someone who needs such help.

Here again, we were trying to be a tad outrageous or very outrageous, depending on your point of view. Some publications actually rejected it because they didn't "get it." We wanted to be funny and attract attention. It your ad doesn't draw a complaint from someone, maybe you aren't making enough of an impression.

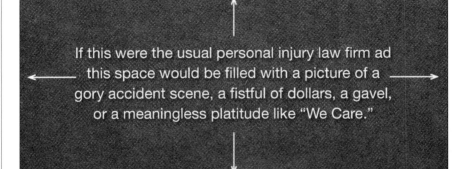

How silly. Most attorney ads do nothing to help you find the best lawyer for your case. We are the only personal injury law firm in Virginia to offer over 400 consumer-friendly videos (**LegalAcademyVideos.com**) and the following books (electronic download or mailed to your home or office before you go for the "free" initial consultation).

Before You Talk To The Insurance Adjuster, Hire An Attorney, or Sign Any Forms

- Free **downloads** at www.FreeLawGuides.com

- Call 703-520-2883 to order **books** *(yes, 100% free and no hassle)*

- Call 703-520-2892 to speak to a *real* **attorney** *(no charge, no stress)*

- Submit your **question** *(free and confidential)* at JustAskBenGlass.com

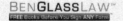

BEN**GLASS**LAW™

Really Cool and Slightly Outrageous
ADVERTISING MATERIAL

I "borrowed" this ad idea from a financial services company; it read something like, "If ours was a typical financial services ad, we'd show you happy people and their yachts and mansions." I liked it and just gave it my own twist to make fun of other lawyers' ads of this nature that offer no useful information. That sets us apart and gives us a leg up in readers' memories. The books I mention, all free info, cover how to choose a lawyer in the lawyer advertising book, what accident victims should *avoid* doing, and settlement options. Settlement options? Yep. Why? First, because some cases are too small. Second, by sending out this book, I'll have made a friend, someone else to receive my newsletter. Third, some will try settling solo but discover their cases are more complex than they thought. So guess who they'll call?

Hey, Accident Victims, if You've Been Injured in an Accident, You're Probably Getting a Lot of Well-Meaning Advice, Aren't You?

From Friends:

"The formula for settling your case is '3x the medical bills'"

"Call Attorney Smith, she handled my divorce and we took him to the cleaners"

"Since you were not at fault, you shouldn't call your own insurance company and report the claim"

From Insurance Adjusters:

"Just sign these forms and give us a statement and we'll take care of you"

"If you don't settle with us soon, we'll just close our file and you won't be able to make a claim"

From Doctors and Chiropractors:

"Since you were in an accident, you aren't allowed to bill your health insurance company – you must use your MedPay or give us cash"

"We've got a treatment plan just for accident victims and we've signed you up for it"

From Lawyers:

"Call us now because folks with lawyers get three times as much in settlements as those who don't hire lawyers (and besides, we care for you!)"

"You need to hire some lawyer right now (and we've got 132 years' combined experience, so it may as well be us)"

Here's Some Advice You Can Take to the Bank

If you have been injured in an accident, then before you (1) talk to the adjuster, (2) hire an attorney or (3) sign any forms, get an instant download of any of these books and watch this short video.

The Accident Book – A consumer guide to surviving the Virginia claim, settlement and litigation process following your accident. (TheAccidentBook.com)

The Truth About Lawyer Advertising – *Your guide to finding the right lawyer for your case, every time.* (TheTruthAboutLawyerAds.com)

Watch this video to find out the things you should know before hiring a personal injury lawyer: 9QuestionsToAsk.com

Want a copy mailed to you instead of getting the instant download? Call [000.000.0000].

In this ad, we offered examples of the advice accident victims regularly hear—get a lawyer, don't get a lawyer, talk to an adjustor, and so on—they will have heard at least one or two of these pieces of advice from others. With our mention of the *Nine Questions to Ask* video, *The Accident Book,* and *The Truth about Lawyer Advertising* book, we were letting them know to contact us before they ever *acted* on any of that advice. We made it as easy as we could for them to get in touch with us rather than the lawyer their doctors or chiropractors are pushing. This ad is heavy on text, but we've learned long text will sell if it's interesting. Those who respond to this ad are, in essence, raising their hands, asking for the free information we're offering, and that's a good first step.

This is an example of a banner ad, which you see so frequently on the Internet. They're a specific size 468 pixels wide by 60 pixels tall (ask your graphic designer about the details). We use these with pay-per-click advertising on the web, so that allows readers to click and download our book.

With this simple but provocative postcard, we were prompting readers to take a particular action—go online to watch our video—as we're really big on education. The "9 Questions to Ask" video gives consumers provocative questions to ask any personal injury attorney they're interviewing. We actually got some hate mail from lawyers who couldn't pass "the test."

ASK THE RIGHT QUESTIONS.
ATTORNEY INTERVIEW CARD

Top 10 Questions to Ask to Find the Perfect Attorney for Your Case

10 Are you board certified? *(You wouldn't let a surgeon operate on you if she wasn't board certified!)*

9 Are you listed in Best Lawyers in America? (BestLawyers.com) *Reputable rating sites*

8 What is your AVVO consumer rating? (Avvo.com)

7 Are you listed in Super Lawyers? (SuperLawyers.com)

Don't fall for the "Submit your case and we'll find you a qualified lawyer" nonsense!

6 Do you have real testimonials? *Hint: "He did a good job." Bob R. Isn't very helpful, is it?*

5 Can your send me your information package before we meet? (Book, CD, DVD) *(No need for a "free consultation" if you can't get a little preview before the meeting.)*

4 Will you give me a full written settlement evaluation before we negotiate with the insurance company? *(This is vital.)*

3 Are you a specialist in the type of case that I have? *(You don't go to a family doctor to treat cancer.)*

2 Do you have a track record of success in cases like mine? *(Each case is different but show me something!)*

1 Will you give me the names of three other attorneys who you would trust with my case? *This is the silver bullet question. Watch the attorney's reaction closely.*

We made this update of the "9 Questions to Ask" postcard by putting in one more question and including the handwritten, red interlining. We wanted our readers to take specific action again: download one of my books (we have them in hard copy, as well), entitled *The Truth About Lawyer Advertising* and *Five Deadly Sins That Can Wreck Your Injury Claim*. We wanted recipients to realize that attorneys are all different, but that they can begin to sort them out by asking these questions rather than just hiring the one with the biggest "Hire Me!" ad.

If you were a personal injury attorney and you weren't nationally board-certified, didn't have a perfect "10" rating on AVVO, weren't listed in Best Lawyers in America *and* Super Lawyers, and didn't have a track record of success and a long list of happy clients, what would you say in your advertising?

Right. "We are aggressive."

www.TheTruthAboutLawyerAds.com

(Instant download!)

I'm a student of history; I've read lot of books about advertising over the years. This one was inspired by the Avis vs. Hertz advertising war, which goes back a few years. Hertz was proud to run in their ads, "We're Number One!" but Avis was just as proud to tout the fact "We're Number Two!" If you were number two and all you could brag about was clean ashtrays, what would you say? Of course! "We have clean ashtrays."

This is actually one ad designed to look like two. The top half drives consumers to a stand-alone landing page which offers a variety of instant downloads. Go ahead try it!

The bottom ad is an ad for the book, *Robbery Without a Gun*. In the ad, we let them know the seven clauses they never want to see in their disability insurance policy, and then we let them know where they can read them, in our book, and a website. Again here, we're offering some information and education readers can receive with a simple response.

198

This is another "three for one" ad, one of which is a totally made up way of poking fun at lawyers, WeNeverLose.com ad. These appear in a tabloid-style newspaper that appears in all the doctors' offices, the ERs, the health spas, and the hair salons in our area. That's where we place a lot of our print ads. Local newspapers are good "targeted" places for professionals to advertise. Check out the format, but also check out the language we use in these.

If you can find a better *Dumfries, VA* personal injury law firm for your serious personal injury case, *USE THEM!*

CATCHY HEADLINE, HUH?

No, we're not saying we are better than anyone else.

(THE REGULATORS WON'T LET ME SAY THAT!)

But what I can say is that you darn well better do your homework before you hire a personal injury lawyer from Dumfries, Virginia for what is likely the most important legal transaction of your life: the handling of your serious personal injury claim.

Surprisingly, most consumers spend more time researching their next refrigerator than they do their lawyer. (Why else would someone respond to an ad that promised "We Care For You"? Gee, wouldn't you expect your lawyer to care for you? OK, so they promised to be "aggressive." Really? That helps you decide?)

The sad truth is that most lawyer advertising gives you very little information upon which to judge whether they are better than the rest. ALL LAWYERS KNOW THAT THERE ARE SOME IN THE COMMUNITY WHO ARE BETTER THAN THE REST.

The only way for you to find out if there is a better law firm than the one running huge TV ads promising "No Fee if No Recovery" is to take the time to educate yourself. I've got three free tools for you:

1 My controversial book *The Truth About Lawyer Advertising* which you can order yourself a free chapter of simply by going to **www.TheTruthAboutLawyerAds.com**

PROBABLY THE BEST PLACE TO START!

2 The cool video where, in 2 ½ minutes I give you 5 great tips for finding the best lawyer for your case. **www.BenGlassLaw.com**

THE VIDEO IS RIGHT ON THE FRONT PAGE

3 Order a sample chapter of our free consumer guide, *The Five Deadly Sins That Can Wreck Your Injury Claim,* by visiting **www.TheAccidentBook.com**

LEARN MORE ABOUT PERSONAL INJURY CLAIMS IN DUMFRIES

BEN GLASS LAW

FREE Books Before You Sign ANY Form

17932 S. Fraley Blvd Suite 400-F
Dumfries, VA 22026
(703) 424-5669
www.BenGlassLaw.com

Check out the video at www.BenGlassLaw.com and my free consumer guides at www.TheTruthAboutLawyerAds.com and www.TheAccidentBook.com

OTHERWISE YOUR REFRIGERATOR MIGHT BE BETTER AT WHAT IT DOES THAN YOUR LAWYER IS AT WHAT HE/SHE DOES.

©2012 Benjamin W. Glass & Assoc, PC.

We got a bit edgy with this ad, not only with its catchy title, but also with that brazen red text, our own commentary on the ad. But there's still that underlying educational theme we rely on. The teaching point here is that while all professions—dentists, physicians, and so on—have advertising rules they abide by, we like to have fun with the rules and aren't shy of getting close to the edge. We still want readers to act—call for an appointment, watch the video, order sample chapters of our books—but we figure an ad like this will make them chuckle, relax, and then call us.

SUGGESTED READING

If you're serious about marketing and building your practice better, read these books:

The Ultimate Marketing Plan, Dan Kennedy

No B.S. Grassroots Marketing, Dan Kennedy and Jeff Slutsky

No B.S. Direct Marketing, Second Edition, Dan Kennedy

Tested Advertising Methods, John Caples

Advertising Secrets of the Written Word, Joseph Sugarman

1,001 Ways to Market Your Books, John Kramer

Endless Referrals, Bob Berg

Hey Whipple, Squeeze This (The Classic Guide to Creating Great Ads), Luke Sullivan

The Referral Engine, John Jantsch

The 100 Greatest Advertisements 1852–1958, Julian Watkins

Read Me (A Century of Classic American Book Advertisements), Dwight Garner

When Advertising Tried Harder (The 60s: The Golden Age of American Advertising), Larry Dobrow

Influence, Science and Practice, Robert Cialdini

The E-Myth, Michael Gerber

A Success System to Building a World Class Law Firm through Effective, Ethical and Outside-the-Box Marketing, Michael Gerber and Ben Glass (available at www. GLMWebstore.com)

Delivering Happiness, a Path to Profits, Passion and Purpose, Tony Hsieh (CEO Zappos)

Think and Grow Rich, Napoleon Hill

EntreLeadership, Dave Ramsey

The One Thing, Gary Keller

The Slight Edge, Jeff Olson

INDEX

C

D

E

F

I

J

K

L

M

N

R

S

T

Would you like to get instant delivery of a set of full color marketing samples that I use in BenGlassLaw?

How about updates or attorney marketing ethics, times news about our upcoming events and new resources for the solo and small firm attorney?

It's easy—

Go to

RegisterThisBook.com
to register your purchase.

ABOUT THE CD ENCLOSED WITH THIS BOOK

The attached CD interview of Ben Glass is an important adjunct to this book because in the interview, Ben digs down into his philosophy on a number of issues including his view of the moral basis for attorney advertising, why understanding capitalism can make you a better marketer, and why viewing your practice as a business, not a "calling," is good for you, your family, your clients and society.

Ben also explains why it is that the solo and small firm lawyers will be the ones who save the legal profession from the venture capitalists who are hell-bent on destroying it as we know it.

We hope you enjoy the CD. More importantly, we hope you act on its suggestions.

(If you purchased an electronic version of the book, or if you would like to download the interview to your device, go to RenegadeLawyerBonus.com and type "vulture" in the space where it asks for a code.)